start simple

Also by Lukas Volger

*Bowl: Vegetarian Recipes for Ramen, Pho,
Bibimbap, Dumplings, and Other One-Dish Meals*

*Vegetarian Entrees That Won't Leave You Hungry:
Nourishing, Flavorful Main Courses That Fill the Center of the Plate*

*Veggie Burgers Every Which Way: Fresh, Flavorful and Healthy
Vegan and Vegetarian Burgers—Plus Toppings, Sides, Buns and More*

HARPER WAVE

Start Simple

Eleven Everyday Ingredients for Countless Weeknight Meals

Lukas Volger

PHOTOGRAPHY BY CARA HOWE   ILLUSTRATIONS BY ALLIRA TEE

HarperCollins books may be purchased for educational, business, or sales promotional use. For information, please email the Special Markets Department at SPsales@harpercollins.com.

FIRST EDITION

Photography by Cara Howe
Illustrations by Allira Tee
Designed by Leah Carlson-Stanisic

Library of Congress Cataloging-in-Publication Data has been applied for.

ISBN 978-0-06-288359-9

20 21 22 23 24 LSC 10 9 8 7 6 5 4 3 2 1

For Max, Casady, Zoe, and Ali

Contents

introduction

My favorite meals often start simple, with a single, promising ingredient that sends me down a sometimes unexpected path to a satisfying dinner. Oftentimes the premise is little more than *Let's see what I've got in my kitchen*. There are eggs, so I'll be fine. A half tub of leftover roasted mushrooms. Some day-old bread. Perfect. This will make a nice strata, a comforting dish that I can load up with sweet caramelized onions, assemble like a frittata on the stovetop, and then pass to the oven where it'll swell just a bit, like a soufflé.

Or maybe there's a block of tofu. Again, I can't go wrong. There's always soy sauce on hand, which, combined with equal parts balsamic vinegar and a jolt of freshly ground black pepper, is the basis for a marinade that transcends the sum of its parts. All that's needed to round it out is some steamed rice, maybe some quickly wilted greens, too. Meanwhile, there's a butternut squash on the counter begging to be put to use. How about I hack that in half, rub it with oil, and roast it in the oven while the tofu does its thing. Then once it's cooled, I'll mash it up and pack it into containers—destined later in the week to be added to a sandwich, or whisked into pancake batter, or stirred into my morning oats. Or a couple sweet potatoes instead. Those always come in handy, making their way into cold salads with yogurt, or to be smeared on grilled bread, or slathered with miso butter while still warm and stuffed with a handful of arugula.

The secret to this kind of cooking, of course, is making sure that there will be ingredients on hand that spark such inspiration, and then having a few ideas for what to do with them once they're at home. And that's what this book is about: manageable and inspiring everyday cooking, with the types of recipes and tools that will help to make everyday cooking a habit.

Cookbooks that aim to unlock the secrets of weeknight cooking usually overwhelm me. The shopping lists, the menus, the loads of prepping that must be done when you might otherwise be enjoying yourself on the weekend. . . . It can be tough to see the forest through the trees, and with that type of plan, I often wonder if the sacrifice is actually outweighed by the reward.

Instead, how about this: Get into the habit of picking up most of these eleven primary ingredients:

winter squash

tofu

hearty greens

beans (canned or dried)

sweet potatoes

eggs

mushrooms

tortillas

cabbage

cauliflower or broccoli

summer squash

My guess is that a number of these items are already fixtures in your shopping basket. Good. Now you just need a pantry stocked with some essentials—nothing obscure or difficult to find (though even experienced cooks will find some new ideas for these ingredients here). Then, when it comes time to cook, you will know that you're armed with the tools needed to make something delicious for yourself, your family, your roommates—and that in most cases, no further planning ahead is required.

This, I've come to learn, is how most good home cooks—the ones who can whip up something on a whim, seemingly from nothing—operate. They don't shop from ingredient lists of recipes, they aren't militant about planning ahead. Instead they know what they like and know what they need—they have their own list of essentials that cumulatively constitute a stocked kitchen—and over time they've developed a knack for what goes with what, or what can be swapped for what. They've developed confidence. When it comes time to figure out what to eat, it isn't often the finished dish that first comes to mind, but that mental snapshot of what's in their fridge. From there, one thing leads to another, and suddenly there's dinner.

Can you turn into one of these cooks overnight? Unfortunately, no. But *Start Simple* will put you onto the right path.

In addition to writing cookbooks, I'm a cook who's spent time in restaurants, food production, food media, and other corners of the food world. But my comfort zone has always been my own kitchen. I like its habits and routines, and I like the whole-life project of it, how there's always something new to learn, to get better at, and to try. But this doesn't mean I enjoy complicated, fussy cooking, though I do enjoy a challenge. And I love hosting dinner parties (who doesn't enjoy an excuse to have the party come to you?). But my favorite kind of cooking is and will always be weeknight food: of-the-moment cooking, the stuff that comes together pretty quickly by assembly of a few components, inspired by what's on hand. Sometimes it can't be re-created, cobbled together as it is from bits of leftovers and odds and ends that are hiding in the fridge. But it's honest cooking, not always wedded to a recipe, lending itself to inspired swaps and substitutions (and as I've learned from reading the comments sections of recipe sites, swaps and substitutions are how people actually cook).

Which is not to say that I want to get rid of recipes, but for the sake of this kind of cooking, I think it's helpful to develop a somewhat different kind of relationship with them. Collected here are indeed recipes, many of them my weeknight go-tos. Follow them and you won't be disappointed. But they also represent a stepping-stone toward learning how to depend less on the recipe itself, and to start flexing your improvisational muscles. Use these recipes and then deviate from them. Mollie Katzen, the influential author of *The Moosewood Cookbook* and many other cookbooks, described it to me when I had the chance to interview her: Mollie's ideal for her readers is that they get to know her recipes and then feel free to make them their own, to "go from here."

I grew up in Boise, Idaho, on a standard American diet—meat and two sides, with a glass of milk. I was well fed, and lucky to have dinner at the table with my parents and brother, Max, most nights. After I left home for college I started learning about the alarming toll (environmental- and animal-welfare-wise) of meat consumption in the United States, and it motivated me toward cutting it from my diet. In the twenty years since, I've fluctuated back and forth from being a strict vegetarian, but a meatless approach has proven to be infinitely inspiring as a cook and satisfying and nourishing as an eater. And what's become a constant is that "weeknight" cooking—my regular, on-the-fly, default cooking—is almost always meatless. In this way, I don't think of vegetarianism as a special or restrictive diet, but as a sensible way to eat most of the time. In my conversations with friends, family, and readers, and from what I observe in other people's shopping and cooking habits, this is a way of eating that's been gaining traction for some time now.

So the chapters in *Start Simple* represent what I think of as the essentials of a pantry, vegetarian or otherwise: primary ingredients that are easy to find, stay fresh for a while, and are inexpensive and versatile in the kitchen. Yes, at the farmers market you could find heirloom and locally sourced versions of all these items, which are likely of better quality, and if you were to exclusively shop seasonally your shopping basket might look different. But in *Start Simple*, shopping at the farmers market isn't the goal (though I encourage you to familiarize yourself with the local markets in your area!). The goal is instead to acknowledge the reality that busy people tend to do most of their shopping at places like Trader Joe's. So for the most part, that's how I've defined the scope of this book.

Within each chapter is a section of recipes meant as a jumping-off point—ways to use roasted, mashed squash or roasted mushrooms, or a collection of distinctive marinades for roasted tofu. These sections aim to help set the tone for the given ingredient and serve to illustrate the modular, or component-oriented, quality that is inherent in cooking with it. If you can step back from a traditional recipe to the point that the ingredient list fades somewhat from view, what's visible instead is a quick assembly of a few components; a primary ingredient or two that's embellished in a few different ways with texture and flavor.

The Brothy Beans on page 74 are a good example of this. In that recipe, I hope to sell you on the glory of a pot of home-cooked beans and the savory liquid they cook in—the bean broth. Serve your home-cooked beans this way, with a drizzle of olive oil. Then in a few of the bean soups or baked bean recipes that follow, you'll see that these brothy beans serve as an ingredient or, rather, a component. In soup recipes, you'll

often soften some aromatic vegetables, like onions, carrots, and celery, then add cooked beans. After that, you'll pour in a measured amount of liquid to cover everything. Here, on the other hand, you add the whole pot of beans and all their liquid. You'll need to see for yourself if the bean broth provided enough liquid for your dish, and if there isn't enough, add more water. In this way, there's not a fixed volume; it has to be assessed by judgment and sensory (in this case, visual) cues. Judgment and sensory cues are at the heart of cooking, the muscles that define a confident cook, and this is one easy exercise to start training them.

And in keeping with the goal of being sensitive to the realities of shopping and weeknight home cooking, I want to share one of my realities that I don't often see reflected in cookbooks: I'm rarely cooking for a four-person nuclear family. This is very much the standard in cookbooks—I think the assumption is two parents (a mom and a dad), two kids, a dog, a picket fence. Not that there's any problem with that (aside from the fence, I grew up this way), but I know that many of us live differently, whether we want to or not. All my adult life, for example, my default has been cooking for one or two people. I've lived alone off and on for years, and now I most often cook for my boyfriend, Vincent, and me. So while halving a recipe or planning for leftovers isn't a huge deal, recipes that serve four aren't always convenient.

In *Start Simple*, I'm pleased to incorporate my cooking reality. While many recipes do bow to convention and serve four, I aimed to include several that serve just one or sometimes two, designed in part for the cooking scenario where many of us give up—when you get home late from work, hungry, wanting to collapse before a Netflix special, just eat scrambled eggs, or eat by hand from a box of cereal, or, worse, order delivery. Here I hope to offer some more exciting options that take minutes to prepare: a greens-stuffed omelet with tahini-yogurt sauce and pickled onions, a bowl of "breakfast beans" with seared scallions and flexible toppings, or a big spinach salad with kimchi, cheddar, and a crispy fried egg.

My hope is that *Start Simple* strengthens your relationship with your kitchen as it is, and that it accommodates the reality of your own busy life. I want to give you the tools to make more—and better—meals without having to dramatically uproot shopping habits or monopolize your free time. But I don't want you to overthink it. By learning to hone a few skills and to trust your instincts, these simple, everyday ingredients will open up a feast of possibilities.

start simple

CHAPTER 1

A Few Kitchen Items That Help Me Love Cooking

I won't bore you by running through a list of what tools and equipment you need to cook—almost every other cookbook has that info for you, plus I think you probably know that you need a few knives and some pots and pans. But there are a couple of not-obvious things that I've come to think of as invaluable.

My Japanese Mandoline

This tool—the inexpensive model made by Benriner is what I have—has earned its modest cost in gold. For slicing onions uniformly thin, for example, you'd need to have excellent knife skills. With a mandoline, anyone can do it. It's also perfect for shaving radishes or slicing cucumbers for pickles. When working with one of these, give the task your full attention and use the finger guard that usually comes in the package, as it's very easy to cut yourself.

My Big, Sturdy Cutting Board

Working on a cutting board that is either too small or so flimsy and lightweight that it's slipping around on the countertop while you work can make cooking both frustrating and dangerous. Find a cutting board that gives you the room you need to work, and that will stay put as you do it. A wood butcher block will last a lifetime with proper care, or head to a restaurant supply store for one of the heavyweight rubber or plastic boards that are common in restaurant kitchens. To prevent your cutting board from sliding around, place a damp towel or paper towel underneath it.

My Chef's Knife

You need a handle that you can grip with your whole hand while the blade is fully in contact with the cutting board—this is not the case with a paring knife or anything the size of a steak knife. A chef's knife is the answer, and I believe it's essential to become confident working with one as your primary slice-and-dice instrument. I also encourage everyone to take a knife skills class at your local culinary education center. If you've never learned the essentials of knife skills—how to properly hold a knife, some of the classic methods for slicing and dicing common foods, and good knife maintenance and care, I firmly believe that nothing will improve your cooking more.

My Rice Cooker

I don't understand why it took me so long to buy a rice cooker. Maybe I wanted to spare my small kitchen another appliance? But as soon as I did buy one, I wished I could have gone back in time and saved myself all the inconsistent saucepans of rice I'd fixed over the years and all that valuable stovetop real estate. A rice cooker makes it perfect every time, is entirely hands off, will keep the rice warm for hours, and can effortlessly cook any number of other grains. If you have a multicooker like an Instant Pot, you've got a rice cooker.

My Small Skillet

I have a small, 6-inch cast-iron skillet, and I use it all the time. Part of its utility for me is the meals-for-one that I cook. It's incredibly useful for toasting spices, reheating sauces, frying or scrambling eggs, searing a veggie burger, making a small frittata or dish of baked eggs, and so much more. It's one of the tools I reach for most frequently.

Olive Oil in a Squeeze

Many chefs I know keep olive oil on the counter in a cheap plastic squeeze bottle, and they know what they're doing. Forget about using a fancy cruet for oil, which always drips down the side and leaves a ring on the counter, and instead just store the big glass bottle or can your oil comes in in a dark and cool place, where it'll be better protected from going rancid. Then, decant a cup or so into a plastic squeeze bottle and leave it on the counter for easy access. It's pleasurable to use, squirting a splash in a skillet or decoratively drizzling over soups and plated salads. Once you try it, you'll know what I mean.

My Toaster Oven

I had a cheap toaster oven for years before I invested in a high-quality one, and the investment has paid off in a major way. I use my Breville toaster oven to toast bread, but also to reheat leftovers (I don't have a microwave, so I scoop leftovers into a small baking dish, cover it with foil, and place it in the toaster oven), roast off a small tray of nuts or spices, bake a small frittata (using my 6-inch skillet) or small dish of baked eggs, and the broiler function often comes in handy for blistering smaller amounts of vegetables like to-matoes or zucchini. In most of these cases, it heats up much more efficiently than my oven does, making for quicker cooking.

My Mortar and Pestle

My mortar and pestle used to be a set piece in my kitchen—I hardly did anything with it at all. But then I learned how to use it properly, and now I can't imagine life without it. The secret to it is that using it shouldn't be a shoulder exercise. You don't need to *force* the mortar or engage your whole body into it. Rather, for pounding whole spices, making sauces and pestos, and—my favorite—pulverizing super-stale bread to very quickly make breadcrumbs, just *tap tap tap* with the pestle, letting gravity and the friction of the mortar against the pestle do its thing. Once everything is coarsely ground, you can introduce a stirring motion to grind its contents even more finely.

My Collection of Cloth Napkins

What an easy way to elevate a typical weeknight dinner at home! They don't need to be nice napkins—you can stock up from the clearance bin at most home supply stores. I keep a good supply so that I don't have to worry about running out, and I just toss them into the laundry basket when I'm done. Similarly, I have a whole basket of kitchen towels in the kitchen, enough of them that I never worry about running out—and they're available for easy access, to be used for cleaning up a spill, pressing a block of tofu dry, or hand washing. Both these items also serve to reduce my paper towel consumption.

CHAPTER 2

A Few Tips That Will Make You a Better Cook

As with any skill or hobby, the only way to become a better cook is by doing it: by trying new things but also repeating some of the same things over and over until you learn them inside out. It's thrilling to develop a close relationship with a dish, to know the precise rhythm and minutiae involved in, say, making an omelet. You can go by feel, waving your hand over the skillet to assess the temperature; working with intent when moving the uncooked eggs around, anticipating what's going to happen next; identifying the exact moment of almost-doneness—when to take the pan off the heat and slide the omelet onto a plate, where residual heat will finish the cooking. You can make a thousand omelets this way, and still there will be some curveballs, new tricks to learn, and new ways to change up the technique and process—which I think is what makes cooking fun. The more experience you accumulate, the better you get at thinking on your feet. If you want to become a better cook, my top advice is just to keep cooking, and to pay closer attention to the process and what you taste. Beyond that, I have a few other tips for cooks who are just beginning to flex their kitchen muscles.

Learn to Trust Your Senses

My recipes almost always include a sensory cue—when the garlic is fragrant, or when the juices are bubbling—in addition to an approximate amount of time for said cue to transpire. The sensory cue is much more important than the suggested time. The conditions of our cooking change greatly from one kitchen to the next: Ovens run hot; vegetables are inconsistent in shape, size, and water content; temperature and humidity affect how some dishes will turn out; low heat on one range top could be medium on another. So start paying less attention to suggested times and paying more attention to your senses—your nose, your eyes, your ears, and your taste buds. This will help you to dial into the alchemy of food, developing your own relationship with it, so that you'll know how to be in control as a cook in spite of ever-changing conditions.

Give Yourself the Space You Need

You don't need a huge kitchen to have space for cooking. Giving yourself space to cook is as much about clearing a dedicated area and getting a big cutting board for vegetable prep as it is about just being the boss. Know what's going to go where. You don't want to be scrambling to figure out where to put a hot baking sheet while it's threatening to burn a hole through your oven mitt. Understand your kitchen's strengths and limitations, and set it up in a way that makes it most functional for you. This is also a reminder to start every cooking project by making sure there aren't any dirty dishes in the sink, and to clean them dutifully as you go.

Take a Knife Skills Class

This one bears repeating: If you're not confident with a chef's knife, there's nothing that will change the way you cook more than a knife skills class. It'll speed up your prep, likely minimize accidents, and make your finished meals even more beautiful. Many home- and kitchen-goods stores offer knife skills classes, as do culinary schools and even continuing education programs at local colleges and universities. And know that it's important that you keep your knives sharp. They should be sharpened professionally or with an at-home sharpener about once a year.

Follow the Recipe—Except When You Don't

If you've ever scrolled the comments section of a recipe website, you know that cooks often, and some-times ambitiously, take liberties with a recipe. Sometimes this is to accommodate an aversion or an al-lergy, or to utilize the ingredients they've already got on hand, or just to customize it to their tastes. I've come to accept this is very common when I get reports from readers—after all, I do it all the time, too. But as you embark on such an off-road adventure, think about food in its base terms. Will your substitution affect texture? If swapping a low-fat item for a high-fat one, it probably will, or a sturdy green like kale for a tender one like spinach, or a gluten-free pasta for a wheat-based one. Or will it affect flavor? Yes, it most likely will! You can anticipate some of these substitutions and leverage your own palate and experience as a cook, but some substitutions, especially when it comes to nondairy or non wheat substitutions in baked goods, can be risky. Just make sure to do a quick Google. There are so many skilled writers and cooks out there who share their knowledge online, and it's very, very likely someone has already attempted your substitution.

Curate Your Pantry

Good cooks have put in the hours cultivating what I think of as a "curated pantry." Similar to the eleven essentials outlined in this book, these pantry items are the paintbrushes and pencils that bring definition to a recipe, if a recipe were a painting. In the past, I would amass a cupboard full of ingredients for one recipe—and never use them again. I hate letting this happen. One strategy to avoid this is to develop a curated approach to what you keep on hand for cooking. Pay attention to what you use most regularly, and work with those items, letting new things in only a few at a time. This isn't to discourage you from trying something new, but rather to help form a solid base for your own culinary sensibility. The recipes here largely draw from a familiar, and a repeating, set of widely available pantry items—vinegars, oils, dried herbs and spices. They also reflect *my* curated pantry.

CHAPTER 3

My Curated Pantry

To cook freely from this book, you'll certainly need some standard pantry items—olive oil, lemons and limes, wine vinegar, salt and pepper, maple syrup, honey, soy sauce, a smattering of vegetables—but there are also a few items I think of as "accent ingredients," which aren't exactly intuitive but have become pantry essentials for me, even if they aren't for you . . . yet.

Kimchi

Kimchi, in particular Napa cabbage kimchi, has been a staple in my pantry for years. Sometimes I make it, sometimes I buy it, but with its lengthy shelf life—it really only gets better with time, in my opinion—I always have it around. If you're unfamiliar, expect a tangy, funky heat, which certainly makes a great addition to a rice bowl but is also great with eggs. If you are vegetarian, check the ingredient list on jarred kimchi carefully, as it may include fish products. A good, and easy-to-find, vegan kimchi is made by Mother-in-Law's.

Castelvetrano Olives

These emerald green olives, about the size of a purple grape, have a slightly firm, buttery texture and a less olive-y taste than many others—in fact, a number of olive-averse people I know make an exception for Castelvetranos. You can buy them jarred or from the olive bar at many supermarkets, and to pit them, place them under the flat side of a chef's knife and firmly press. This'll puncture the fruit (olives are a fruit) and make it possible to pull out the pit.

Tahini

Thank goodness that this Middle Eastern sesame paste has become so popular! I used to think of it only as an ingredient in hummus, but I've come to learn that it has a multitude of other uses: in dressings and sauces, in soups and spread over toast, in desserts and baked goods, and straight off the spoon. Its flavor is a brilliant, fascinating foil, seeming to do it all—its earthiness tempers the sweetness of, say, sweet potatoes, and its sweetness tempers the earthiness of raw mushrooms, for example. My favorite brand is the Whole Foods 365 brand, with the green lid. But whatever brand you pick up, try for the freshest possible, which will taste best, and the solids and oils are less likely to have separated so the tahini will require less stirring.

Good Bread

In the wake of the crusade against gluten, my own bread intake has taken a hit, even though I don't have an allergy. No longer do I have bread with every meal, or even buy it on a regular basis. But when I eat bread, I make it count by eating *good* bread: stuff that's made locally and purchased at peak freshness from the bakery, farmers market, or grocery store. My preference is for naturally leavened and made from whole grains. When I get it home, I slice most of it up, pack it into a resealable bag, and keep it in the freezer. It doesn't take long to defrost sitting out in the kitchen, and you can also put it straight from the freezer into the toaster.

Scallions

Ever since I read about scallions as "jewels of nutrition hiding in plain sight" in the *New York Times* several years ago—they're incredibly rich in phytonutrients, and one of the few vegetables that hasn't undergone extensive breeding (and diminishment of nutrients) to make them more friendly to refrigerated trucks and long trips—I've been very happy to add them to my shopping basket on the regular. Both the white and the green parts are edible. And as you'll see in these recipes, I *love* to cook scallions by roasting, searing, or grilling them. They've got a deep, mature flavor that adds depth to vegetarian dishes.

Vegetable Bouillon Base

Bouillon is just concentrated vegetable stock in a dried format that can be quickly reconstituted with hot water. After years of making my own vegetable stock—which is not hard, and makes great use of vegetable scraps, but can be somewhat time-consuming—I began warming to the Better Than Bouillon brand when making certain soups. It's not a dried boullion, but a paste, and it's just . . . easy. While I'll also frequently use water instead of stock, it's inarguable that stock has backbone, and in some soups—those in which the lead ingredients, such as cauliflower, are on the milder side—you need a bit more support. It's in those cases when I reach for the bouillon. It's quite salty, so I use about half of what the package calls for: ½ teaspoon per 1 cup water.

Miso Paste

Miso is made from fermented soybeans, and its flavor, in my mind, is quintessential umami. It can be a real lifesaver in vegetarian cooking, where such flavors sometimes can be hard to find. It comes in a rainbow of different shades, and generally the darker the miso the stronger and saltier it is. I use it a lot in marinades and spreads, and of course in soup, and even, here in this book, in dessert. I most frequently use light-colored miso pastes.

Fresh Herbs

My ideal self always uses up fresh herbs, strewing them here and there in my daily cooking and pounding anything that's left into pesto that I'll freeze in ice cube trays and squirrel away for a future meal that needs enlivening. But the reality is that I still have trouble working through my herbs before they start to turn slimy. So, here a few things I've learned. One, I now almost always buy just one bunch of herbs for a shopping trip, rather than a couple, and make that one herb assume the full workload of my week's cooking. So many herbs are interchangeable, and using, say, cilantro where you'd typically use parsley or mint, may not always sound logical, but by having a "mint week" or a "dill week," you can learn a lot from seemingly unorthodox flavor profiles. Two, I use them in abundance rather than judiciously, sprinkling them generously over soups, stir-fries, and baked vegetable dishes. I'll treat herbs like parsley, basil, mint, and cilantro like salad greens, leaving them whole and tossing them with lettuce; this really brings their fresh flavors to the forefront. Three, the absolute best way to store herbs is to layer or roll the washed-and-dried herbs in a clean paper towel or kitchen towel, tuck the bundle into a resealable bag, and place it in your refrigerator. They'll keep for up to a week this way.

Cherry Tomatoes

Fresh tomatoes are so, so much better in the peak of summer that it's a waste to bother buying them at any other time of the year. The exception is cherry tomatoes, which don't quite rival a juicy ripe one just plucked off the vine, but are light years ahead of the flavor and texture of a mealy and bland off-season hothouse tomato from the grocery store. I eat cherry tomatoes all year long, fresh in salads and on sandwiches, or broiled or blistered to make a sauce. They always bring a little sunshine to an otherwise wintry meal.

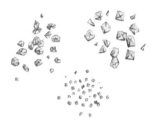

A Note about Salt

My primary cooking salt is Diamond Crystal kosher salt, and then for finishing, I use Maldon salt flakes. Morton's kosher salt has finer, and denser, granules than Diamond Crystal and weighs more—it's almost twice as salty as Diamond Crystal. If Morton's is what you use you'll want to scale back the salt measurements by about 50 percent and then, as always, season to taste. Fine-grain sea salt is 20 percent saltier teaspoon for teaspoon, so for the recipes in this book, use a scant ¼ teaspoon less for each teaspoon. Maldon finishing salt is primarily for texture; you can use another flaky salt or fleur de sel as well. I recommend sticking with a cooking salt you like, be it sea salt or a specific brand of kosher salt. Over time, you'll develop a relationship with it and be able to go by feel.

CHAPTER 4

A Big Winter Squash

When I'm shopping, I often want to load up on winter squash just for the sake of having them to look at on the kitchen counter. With so many varieties, all in their own elegant shapes, stripes, and colors—think butternut and honeynut, acorn and calabaza, pumpkin and delicata, not to mention the dozens of heirloom squash that show up seasonally at the farmers markets—each one is a statement piece.

But, of course, I put them to work. They all require different cooking times and have different finished textures, but most of the winter squash you can find at a grocery store or farmers market is interchangeable in recipes. The real exception is spaghetti squash, which turns into its namesake strands once cooked, and the cooking method for delicata deviates from the others enough that it needs special treatment. (Spaghetti and delicata squash are technically related to zucchini and other summer squash, but their flavors, textures, and cooking methods are associated with their winter cousins.) But for the others, the cooking process is largely the same: Hack them in half and roast. You can scoop out the seeds before or after cooking.

Most everyone I know hates peeling these squash. While some cooks insist that their skins are edible—and in the cases of delicata and kabocha, they indeed are—that doesn't always mean their fibrous, sometimes woody textures make them pleasant to eat. A vegetable peeler usually does the trick for a butternut squash; or you could cut it in half at the neck and, with the flat surface keeping it steady on the cutting board, trim the skin off in downward strokes using a sharp chef's knife. But rather than trying to peel them when they're raw, I most often cook them in their skins and then either scoop out the flesh with a spoon or trim off the peel using a paring knife when the flesh is tender and easier to work with.

Or feel free to grab the peeled and pre-cut packages of squash that many grocery stores now sell and forgo all the worry about skins. For grated squash, such as in the Baked Squash Risotto on page 27, these cubes are easy to send through the feeding tube of a food processor fitted with its grating attachment. For the Ghee-Roasted Butternut Squash with Spiced Honey on page 28, you may need to cut them into smaller pieces.

As these recipes attest, I'm most often drawn to the crowd-pleasing, widely available butternut squash, and, when it's in season, the quick-cooking, no-peeling-required delicata squash. I begin the chapter with my preferred roasting method for winter squash, and the straightforward recipes that follow offer a range of dishes, from salads, risotto, sandwiches, and oatmeal to a simple side dish that allows the vegetable to shine on its own.

This is my favorite way to cook most types of winter squash—halved through the stem, first roasting flat-side down, which initiates the cooking by steaming, and then flipping it over so that the excess liquid cooks off. Then, by coarsely mashing, seasoning, and storing the squash to use later in the week, you've got an ingredient that'll yield more types of dishes than would be easily available to you if you were to have cubed and roasted leftover squash. It's a spread, a sandwich filling, sweet component of a frittata, the starting point of an easy appetizer. Think of it as a more textured, fresher-tasting take on canned sweet potato or squash. For the purposes of the recipes in this section, butternut squash, with its less starchy texture and mild-sweet flavor, is the best one to use. A starchier squash, like acorn or kabocha, will give a different texture to finished dishes.

Roasted, Mashed Butternut Squash

MAKES 2 TO 3 CUPS MASHED SQUASH

1 medium butternut squash, 3 to 4 pounds, or other similar squash

Olive oil
Salt

Preheat the oven to 400°F.

Cut the squash in half lengthwise through the stem. (Don't bother scooping out the seeds.) Rub the squash halves all over with olive oil and place each piece on a baking sheet, cut-side down. Roast for 25 minutes, then flip the squash and continue cooking until tender all over, another 10 to 30 minutes—you should be able to pierce the neck of the squash with a paring knife and meet very little resistance. Allow to cool, then scoop out the seeds and discard them. Use a spoon to scoop all of the flesh into a bowl and discard the skins. Coarsely mash the squash with a spoon or fork and season with salt. Packed in an airtight container, it will keep in the refrigerator for 3 to 4 days.

My beloved 6-inch cast-iron skillet is often put to use to make a frittata like this—it's the right size for a hearty meal for one or a lighter one for two with a salad served alongside. With mashed squash on hand, it comes together in about five minutes. And unlike the Anything Frittata on page 125 (or most frittatas that I make, for that matter), this one isn't studded with chunks of different fillings, but instead has a soft texture, with the mashed squash blending in with the egg. It's also a perfect component in a packed lunch, eaten cold, at room temperature, or reheated if you like. Triple the recipe to make it in a 10-inch skillet.

Butternut Squash Frittata

SERVES 1 TO 2

3 eggs
⅓ cup Roasted, Mashed Butternut Squash
   (page 16)
1 tablespoon grated Parmesan cheese
1 swipe lemon zest
¼ teaspoon salt
Freshly ground black pepper

1 tablespoon butter, divided
1 medium shallot, or ½ small onion,
   minced
Pinch dried thyme
Flaky salt
Olive oil, for drizzling (optional)

Preheat the oven (or a toaster oven!) to 350°F. In a small bowl, whisk together the eggs, squash, cheese, lemon zest, salt, and a few grinds of black pepper.

Melt ½ tablespoon of the butter in a 6-inch skillet over medium heat, then add the shallot and thyme. Cook until softened and translucent, 3 to 5 minutes, then stir them into the bowl with the eggs. Return the pan to the stove and let it reheat. Melt in the remaining ½ tablespoon butter, then pour in the eggs (if your skillet isn't well seasoned, you may need more butter). The eggs should immediately sizzle and cook along the edges of the pan. Use a rubber spatula to stir from the center but without scraping the bottom of the pan. Tuck the spatula underneath a cooked edge, tilting the pan to allow some of the uncooked egg to flow underneath. Repeat this process, working your way around the pan at 90-degree increments for about 2 minutes, at which point the perimeter of the frittata will be mostly set.

Transfer the pan to the oven and cook until just set in the center, about 10 minutes more. Let sit for 5 minutes, then run a spatula around the outside of the frittata to loosen it from the pan, and slide it onto a plate. Serve warm, at room temperature, or cold, with a sprinkle of flaky salt and drizzle of olive oil, if you like.

Intended to be slathered on crackers or toasted or grilled bread, this attractive dip is such an easy appetizer, side dish, or snack. You absolutely want to use good-quality, fresh ricotta, and it's best when both the squash and the ricotta have come to room temperature. For a vegan version, a mild-flavored nut-based ricotta (made from almonds or cashews) makes an excellent substitution, and maple syrup can be swapped for the honey.

Squash and Ricotta Dip

SERVES 6 AS AN APPETIZER OR SIDE

1 cup Roasted, Mashed Butternut Squash
   (page 16)
Kosher salt
1 cup good-quality, fresh ricotta cheese
1 to 2 tablespoons olive oil
1 to 2 tablespoons honey

Juice from ½ lemon, to taste
Flaky salt
Freshly ground black pepper
Crackers or toasted or grilled bread,
   for serving

Ensure that your squash is seasoned well, adding a pinch or two more kosher salt if needed. On a medium platter or salad plate, dollop the squash and ricotta decoratively all over so that they create something of an abstract collage, then use a spoon or dinner knife to swirl them together a bit. Drizzle with the olive oil and honey and finish with a spritz of lemon, a sprinkle of flaky salt, and several grinds of black pepper. Serve with crackers or toasted or grilled bread.

Any sweet, roasted, mashable squash can be incorporated into pancakes, adding some heartiness, nutrition, and more complex flavor to a dish that can often be a little one-note. I like the texture when coarsely mashed squash is used here, but if you don't, make sure to mash up the squash to a smooth consistency before adding it. And if you've got a medley of alternate grain flours, here's a good place to play around with them, substituting up to ½ cup of the all-purpose flour with whole-wheat, spelt, or barley flour, for example.

Squash Pancakes

MAKES 8 TO 10 PANCAKES

1¼ cups all-purpose flour (see headnote)
2 teaspoons baking powder
½ teaspoon salt
A few swipes from a whole nutmeg
1 cup milk
½ cup Roasted, Mashed Butternut Squash
   (page 16)

1 tablespoon melted butter
1 tablespoon maple syrup, plus more
   for serving
1 large egg
½ teaspoon finely grated orange zest
Butter or neutral-tasting oil, for cooking

Preheat the oven to 250°F.

Whisk together the flour, baking powder, salt, and nutmeg in a large bowl. In a separate bowl, whisk together the milk, squash, melted butter, maple syrup, egg, and orange zest. Pour the wet ingredients into the dry and whisk to combine in a few assertive strokes, taking care not to overmix.

Heat a griddle or skillet over medium-high heat, then add a good pat of butter or film of oil. When the foaming subsides, ladle in ¼-cup mounds of batter into the pan, only as many as will fit comfortably without spreading into each other. Cook for 2½ to 3 minutes, until air bubbles gurgle up in the centers of the pancakes, then flip and continue cooking on the other side, another 90 seconds or so. Add more butter to the pan, then proceed cooking more pancakes until you've used all the batter. As the pancakes are cooked, transfer them to a baking sheet or heatproof plate and keep warm in the oven. Serve immediately, with butter and maple syrup if that's your preference.

CANDY YOUR PANCAKES

Working in batches, return the cooked pancakes to the hot skillet, and then pour maple syrup over them, however much you'd typically use at the table. The syrup will bubble and thicken slightly and cling to the crispy edges of the pancakes like a candy coating. It's pretty great. I bypass additional butter at the table (since they're cooked in butter), but I love to finish my maple-coated pancakes with a judicious pinch of flaky salt.

I can't imagine a better thing to eat on a cold night than this sandwich, a vegetarian spin on a croque monsieur: sweet roasted squash marries with creamy béchamel and nutty cheese in a fork-and-knife sandwich for the books. It's inspired by Jody Williams's amazingly good Croque Forestier in her cookbook, *Buvette*. If you have any cooked greens on hand, such as the Marinated Greens on page 54, you can substitute them for the kale. And choose a nice sourdough or sturdy sandwich bread, one that's got some structure. You'll need it to support all the hearty fillings and to keep this sandwich intact.

Croque Courge

MAKES 4 SANDWICHES

Olive oil

1 small bunch kale, stemmed and chopped, or 5 ounces baby kale

2 tablespoons butter

2 tablespoons all-purpose flour

½ teaspoon dried sage

Pinch red pepper flakes

1 cup whole milk

Salt

½ cup Roasted, Mashed Butternut Squash (page 16)

8 slices good-quality sandwich bread, ½ to ¾ inch thick

1 cup grated Gruyère or other nice-melting, assertive Alpine cheese

Fried eggs, for topping (optional)

Preheat the oven to 400°F.

Heat a splash of oil in a medium saucepan over medium heat and add the kale and a few splashes of water if the leaves are dry. Cover and cook for a minute or two, until the greens begin to collapse, then remove the lid and cook, moving them around a bit, until wilted. Drain off the liquid, then transfer to a plate to cool. When safe to handle, squeeze out as much excess liquid as you can, then coarsely chop the greens. Wipe out the pan and return it to the heat.

To make the béchamel, add the butter to the pan (or a small saucepan if you've got premade Marinated Greens, page 54) and melt it over medium heat, then sprinkle in the flour, sage, and red pepper flakes and stir constantly with a small whisk or wooden spoon until the mixture darkens a shade and smells a bit nutty, less than 2 minutes. Pour in the milk, again whisking constantly, and continue to cook until it's simmering around the edges and thickens enough to coat the back of a spoon, 2 to 3 more minutes. Remove from the heat and season with salt.

Arrange the bread slices on a baking sheet and spread 2 tablespoons of the béchamel over each slice. Spread 4 of them with about 2 tablespoons of the squash, followed by ¼ cup of the grated cheese and about ¼ cup of the wilted greens. Place the remaining 4 slices on top, béchamel-side up. The sandwiches can be assembled up to 2 hours before cooking.

Bake for 12 to 15 minutes, until the cheese is melted and the topping is beginning to brown. Turn the broiler to high and place the sandwiches inside. Cook just for a minute or two, watching carefully, until golden brown and bubbling. Top each sandwich with a fried egg, if using. Serve hot, with a knife and fork.

I try to make a big batch of steel-cut oats early in the week, ready to reheat for breakfast in the days that follow. This is a favorite autumnal way of topping it, which helps to keep an old standby interesting through all the weeks of the year. Rather than stirring the squash into the full pot of oatmeal, you can add it to individual bowls, treating it as a topping—a few heaping tablespoons per serving, as pictured.

Steel-Cut Oats with Squash and Tahini

SERVES 4

For the oatmeal

2 tablespoons dairy butter or vegan butter

1 cup steel-cut oats

1 cup whole or unflavored, unsweetened nondairy milk

3 cups water

½ teaspoon salt

1 cup Roasted, Mashed Butternut Squash (page 16)

For serving

Well-stirred tahini

Maple syrup

Brown sugar

Flaky salt

Melt the butter in a medium saucepan over medium heat, then add the oats. Cook, stirring often, until they smell toasty and have darkened a shade, 3 to 4 minutes. Watch that they don't burn. Pour in the milk and water and add the salt. Bring to a boil, then stir once, partially cover the pan, and reduce to a gentle simmer. Cook for 20 minutes. Stir in the squash, then remove from the heat. (The oatmeal will thicken as it cools; stir in additional water or milk when reheating.)

To serve, spoon the hot oatmeal into bowls. For each serving, drizzle with 1 to 2 tablespoons tahini, 1 to 2 teaspoons maple syrup, a small spoonful of brown sugar, and a good pinch of flaky salt.

Despite many attempts, stuffed squash—that ever-enduring vision for a vegetarian holiday main dish, where the hollow of a winter squash is filled with something and then baked—just never works for me. The proportions aren't right, often with too much squash and not enough filling, and it always seems to be the case that either the squash is undercooked or the filling is dried out. Here's my solution: Separately roast long delicata squash "boats" and then add the filling (which can be any grain salad you please). You can also use any other kind of winter squash: Just spoon the salad over quarters or eighths (depending on its size) of nicely cooked winter squash. Even though they won't always look like stuffed squash "boats," they'll still be an improvement on the traditional method.

Deconstructed Stuffed Squash

SERVES 4

2 delicata squash
Olive oil
Salt
2 shallots, diced
¾ cup farro
1 small radicchio, or 3 small heads endive, chopped

¼ cup toasted hazelnuts, pecans, or almonds
¼ cup crumbled blue cheese
¼ cup whole parsley leaves
Juice from ½ lemon, to taste

Preheat the oven to 425°F.

Trim the ends off the squash and then half them lengthwise. Use a spoon to scoop out (and discard) the seeds, then cut each piece in half lengthwise—you'll have 4 pieces. Coat well with olive oil and sprinkle with salt, then arrange upright in a baking dish and roast until tender, 30 to 40 minutes.

Meanwhile, warm a splash of olive oil in a medium saucepan over medium heat. Add the shallots and ½ teaspoon salt and cook until just translucent, 3 to 4 minutes. Stir in the farro, then add 1 cup water. Bring to a simmer, cover, lower the heat, and cook gently for 10 to 20 minutes, until the farro is tender. If there's any liquid left in the pan, drain it off. While the grain is still hot, stir in the radicchio or endive so that it wilts, then add the nuts, cheese, and parsley. Season with salt and spritzes of lemon juice.

To serve, spoon the grain salad over the squash, using the squash hollows as a rough guide. Drizzle with a bit more olive oil and a sprinkle of salt. Serve hot, warm, or at room temperature.

If cooking risotto in the oven is new to you, it will be a revelation—it allows you to bypass the near-constant stirring that the dish usually entails. Here grated squash cooks along with the rice, breaking down a bit and enriching the dish with plenty of flavor. If you have homemade vegetable stock, use that here in place of all or some of the water. I generally find that water is a better liquid than any store-bought broth for risotto—those stocks muddy the delicate flavor of the rice. The salad greens that top the dish, which soften slightly as they integrate into the risotto, offer an extra dose of vegetables and a pop of color and turn this risotto into a main course.

Baked Squash Risotto

SERVES 4

3 tablespoons butter or olive oil, divided
1 medium onion, or 2 leeks, white parts
    only, chopped
Salt
2 cloves garlic, minced
3 cups winter squash grated on the large
    holes of a box grater (about 12 ounces)

1 cup Arborio rice
4 cups hot water, divided
½ cup dry white wine
⅓ cup finely grated Parmesan cheese
4 handfuls tender greens, such as baby
    spinach, baby arugula, or baby kale
Olive oil

Preheat the oven to 325°F.

In a deep, oven-safe skillet or Dutch oven that has a lid, melt (or warm) 2 tablespoons of the butter or olive oil over medium heat. Add the onion and ½ teaspoon salt and cook until softened and translucent, 5 to 7 minutes. Raise the heat and add the garlic, followed by the squash. Cook, stirring often, until fragrant, another 3 to 4 minutes. Add the rice, stir, and then add 2½ cups of the hot water and another ½ teaspoon salt. Stir again, then cover the pot and transfer to the oven.

Bake until the rice is pleasantly tender and much of the liquid is absorbed, 20 to 25 minutes. Remove from the oven and stir in the wine, the remaining 1 tablespoon butter or olive oil, and the cheese, stirring thoroughly until you've got an appealingly loose—not sticky or gloppy—risotto. Taste and add ¼ teaspoon more salt if needed.

Quickly toss the tender greens with a bit of olive oil and a pinch of salt. Divide the risotto among serving bowls and top each serving with a handful of dressed greens. Serve immediately.

Roasting butternut squash using not olive oil but ghee—butter from which the milk solids have been strained out, which allows the squash to roast without the fat burning—adds a glorious richness and depth. Try using ghee in place of olive oil when roasting beets, potatoes, and other varieties of winter squash as well, to make them more flavorful and luscious, or as a cooking fat when making soups. Drizzled with honey, this squash treatment is vegetable candy. If you don't have the time or inclination to procure ghee, substitute olive oil, but don't skip the broiling step.

Ghee-Roasted Butternut Squash with Spiced Honey

SERVES 4 AS A SIDE

1 medium butternut squash
    (about 2 pounds), peeled, seeded,
    and cut into ½-inch cubes
2 tablespoons ghee (store-bought or
    homemade, recipe opposite), melted

3 tablespoons honey
¼ teaspoon smoked paprika
½ teaspoon dried thyme
Salt
Freshly ground black pepper

Preheat the oven to 375°F. Line a baking sheet with parchment paper.

In a large bowl, coat the cubed squash in the melted ghee, then spread in an even layer on the prepared baking sheet. Transfer to the oven and roast until tender, stirring periodically, about 25 minutes.

Combine the honey with the smoked paprika and thyme in a small saucepan over low heat and warm it just enough to make it loose and runny.

Drizzle the spiced honey over the warm squash and stir with a spatula to coat evenly. Turn your broiler to high and place the squash beneath it. Cook for 3 to 4 minutes—the squash will blister in spots, which is what you want. Season with salt and black pepper and serve warm or at room temperature.

GHEE

In ghee, butter is essentially concentrated, with the water cooked out, and the milk solids have cara-melized to lend nutty and toasty notes. It brings a distinctive richness to whatever it touches. With the milk solids removed, some people with light dairy intolerances can digest ghee without issue, and it's also shelf stable and keeps for a very long time. And in high-heat cooking, where butter and even olive oil will burn, ghee's delicious flavor stays the course. Store-bought ghee is an excellent, flavor-boosting ingredient to keep on hand. Just make sure to choose one in which the ingredient list includes only clarified butter (sometimes they're flavored with different spices, too). But it's also very easy to make your own.

To make ghee: Melt two sticks of unsalted butter in a small saucepan over medium-low heat. Cook for about 20 minutes, gently swirling the pan every now and then. White foam will collect on the surface and the liquid will bubble aggressively, which is the water is cooking off. Continue cooking until the bubbling begins to subside somewhat and the milk solids sink to the bottom of the pan. Watch for them to take on a reddish-brown color, and once they do, strain the fat through a cheesecloth-lined sieve or coffee filter into a heat-safe jar. Cool completely, then seal and store in the cupboard or the fridge. It'll keep there for months. *Makes about 1 cup*

While vastly more weeknight-friendly than a traditional lasagna, I think it's helpful, in terms of managing expectations, to distinguish a skillet lasagna as more akin to other types of pasta prepared on the stovetop than its baked counterpart—which is to say, it's a bit loose. This is not a bad thing, and no one I know has ever complained about melty strands of cheese and savory tomato sauce making a delicious mess of tender noodles and various vegetable fillings on the plate. (It does firm as it cools, and becomes easy to slice into slabs.) I encourage you to use this recipe as a blank canvas for any number of additions, starting with dollops of Roasted, Mashed Butternut Squash (page 16); Roasted Mushrooms (page 136); and/or little piles of Marinated Greens (page 54). If you'd like to make the lasagna vegan, use a vegan butter (I like the Miyoko's brand of cultured European-style butter) or olive oil for the butter; an unflavored, unsweetened nondairy milk; and you can either omit the cheese—it's still plenty rich without it—or use spoonfuls of a vegan ricotta or mozzarella in place. And make sure that your pesto is cheese-free.

A Stovetop Lasagna

SERVES 4 TO 6

2 tablespoons butter
2 cloves garlic, minced
2 tablespoons all-purpose flour
1 cup whole milk
One 28-ounce can crushed tomatoes
1 teaspoon salt
Freshly ground black pepper
8 ounces no-boil lasagna noodles
    (10 to 12 sheets)*

2 tablespoons pesto, store-bought or
    homemade (page 128)
8 ounces mozzarella cheese, cut or torn
    into small pieces, or 2 cups shredded
Up to 1½ cups additional building block
    fillings: Roasted, Mashed Butternut
    Squash (page 16); Roasted Mushrooms
    (page 136), Marinated Greens (page 54)

Melt the butter in a deep skillet or Dutch oven (no more than 10 inches in diameter) over medium heat. Stir in the garlic, and when fragrant, add the flour. Stir constantly for a minute or two, until the mixture darkens a shade, then while continuing to stir, add the milk in a steady stream, followed by the tomatoes. Bring to a simmer and cook for about 10 minutes, until slightly thickened. Add the salt and many grinds of black pepper. Remove the pan from the heat.

Use a wooden spoon or spatula to gently press one-third of the noodles into the sauce, breaking them as necessary to approximate a single layer. Add dollops of half of the pesto and sprinkle with one third of the cheese, as well as half of any of the optional additions you may be using. Repeat with another layer of lasagna noodles and fillings, then make a final layer of noodles, pressing gently on them to ensure that no dry noodle is exposed. Scatter the remaining cheese over the top.

(If you don't have a deep skillet, use a 10-inch skillet, but after preparing the sauce, transfer it to a bowl, and then, in the empty skillet, assemble the lasagna the traditional way—a spoonful of sauce in the bottom of the pan, followed by a layer of noodles, followed by sauce, pesto, cheese, and so on. It will likely still all fit in the skillet, but this way you'll know for sure if it doesn't.)

Return to the heat and bring to a simmer. Cover with a lid or piece of aluminum foil and cook for 12 minutes. Uncover and simmer for 5 minutes more to dry out the surface a bit. Test for doneness by inserting a paring knife into the noodles. Remove from the heat and let cool, uncovered, for at least 10 minutes before serving.

* You can also use standard (not no-boil) noodles; soak them in hot water for a few minutes, stirring a few times to prevent them from congealing, until they're just pliable. Drain the noodles and set aside until ready to use.

STOVETOP LASAGNA,
PAGE 30

A Block of Tofu

Nutritionist and author Marion Nestle, my favorite authority on food and nutrition, says that the studies that elicit tofu fear and confusion are "painfully inconsistent . . . not least because so much of the research is sponsored by industries with a vested interest in its outcome." She advises that we regard tofu not as a miracle food, as it's often framed in the context of vegan and vegetarian diets, but as "a food"—one to incorporate into your diet with an eye toward balance. I feel this way about most ingredients.

What's also interesting about the soy debates is the parallel narrative of how soybeans have been greatly industrialized—and subsidized—for processed food production here in the United States. In these processed foods, soybeans appear as soy protein isolate, a highly concentrated form of soy made from the bean's protein (and the phytoestrogens contained in it). To make it, the soybeans are stripped of all the carbohydrates, fiber, fat, omega-3s, and minerals that would otherwise make them a whole and nutritionally dense ingredient. To get the full benefits of soybeans for the amount of soy protein isolate that appears in, say, processed soy milks, many frozen veggie burgers, and protein powders, you'd have to eat a *lot* of soybeans.

Tofu, compared to these soy isolate things, is hardly processed at all and utilizes the whole soybean. Made from just soybeans and a coagulant, it retains the bean's rich balance of macronutrients. While I don't eat tofu every day, I enjoy it often and without any worry. It's delicious, hearty, versatile, and an easy component for a nourishing meal. Tofu can be one part of a more complicated dish—a curry, or a soup, or a stir-fry—or it can be the primary ingredient, as it is for most of the recipes in this chapter, baked in a flavorful marinade or served under a quick, saucy stew of fresh tomatoes spiked with soy sauce (page 46).

The assortment of baked tofu recipes that start this chapter demonstrate simple ways to pack it with flavor, and offer an alternative to those vacuum-packed parcels of baked and marinated tofu available at the grocery store (though those can be a lifesaver sometimes). Accompanied by some cooked grain, steamed or roasted vegetables, or a simple green salad, you've got a balanced meal right there at your fingertips. Others in this chapter, such as the Breakfast Tofu Scramble on page 45, marry the tofu with full servings of vegetables to make a meal on their own. If you're a tofu skeptic, I hope these recipes will sway you. In my kitchen, it's a valuable weeknight building block.

If you like dishes that bridge the sweet-savory divide, you'll love the whole orange in this marinade. It adds a chewy, candied element to the tofu, where the slight bitterness of the rind pairs beautifully with the gentle sesame note. Do your best to slice the orange very thinly, as it can be a bit overwhelming if it's cut in too-large chunks. A sharp chef's knife will do the trick.

Honey-Orange Tofu

SERVES 3 OR 4

½ medium sweet orange, any variety
2 tablespoons olive oil
2 tablespoons white wine vinegar
2 tablespoons honey
1 teaspoon toasted sesame oil

¾ teaspoon salt
Freshly ground black pepper
One 15-ounce block firm tofu, blotted dry
    and cut into 8 slabs

Preheat the oven to 400°F.

Trim the ends off the orange and then cut into quarters through the stem. Laying a flat surface on your cutting board, slice each quarter into very thin—⅛ inch thick or less—quarter rings. If you come across any seeds, discard them. Yes, you're leaving the peel on!

In a small bowl, whisk together the olive oil, vinegar, honey, sesame oil, salt, and several grinds of black pepper, then stir in the orange pieces.

Arrange the tofu pieces in a baking dish—one in which they fit in a snug single layer (an 8 x 8 inch or 7 x 11 inch works well)—then pour the marinade over the top, flipping the pieces to coat. Transfer to the oven and bake for about 40 minutes, flipping the tofu halfway through, until well bronzed and the oranges are slightly caramelized. Serve hot.

THE GROCERY STORE

The range of tofu options can be a little confusing if you're new to tofu—or even if you're not. Here's a quick rundown.

Blocks of firm tofu for roasting, pan-searing, or even mashing into crumbles are typically sold in plastic pouches or bins and submerged in water. There is usually "firm" and "extra firm" available, and sometimes "medium" as well. Go with firm or extra firm, as these are less likely to fall apart as they cook. This style of tofu needs to be drained and then blotted or pressed dry with a clean kitchen towel or a few paper towels.

You can extract even more of the liquid by wrapping it in a clean kitchen towel, placing a skillet or baking pan on top, and then adding something heavy (cans of beans or tomatoes, or, as I do, my heavy mortar) to weigh it down; let it stand for 20 minutes or even a few hours to really dry out. This is necessary for making crispy fried tofu, but for baking and sautéing, the idea is that by extracting the water you're making room for flavorful marinades.

Hodo, a Bay Area–based manufacturer, sells firm tofu in vacuum-sealed pouches, and it is exceptionally good—I'll slice it up right out of the package and eat it like cheese. It's denser than any water-packed, grocery store tofu I've ever tried, and since it's not packed in water, it doesn't need to be pressed.

While sometimes you'll find silken tofu alongside regular tofu in the refrigerated dairy or produce section, more often it's sold in shelf-stable Tetra Paks in the same section of the grocery store as the soy sauce and other Asian ingredients. Silken tofu isn't pressed—it has a higher water content and custardy consistency (it's often served topped with a sweet syrup as dessert). You can carefully slice it into cubes for soups, like the Miso Soba Bowl with Greens and Mushrooms on page 142, or slabs, like the Silken Tofu with Soy-Sauced Tomatoes on page 46.

PINEAPPLE-SRIRACHA
TOFU, PAGE 41

HONEY-ORANGE
TOFU, PAGE 36

MISO-MAPLE TOFU
WITH MELTED ONIONS
PAGE 40

If you're a fan of caramelized onions (who's not?) the "melted onions" here—flavored with savory miso paste and a bit of maple syrup—will be right up your alley. Make sure to slice the onions very thinly in order for them to properly "melt," ideally using a mandoline if you have one. In the oven, they're going to pool in their own juices and reduce to a jammy consistency, clinging to the tofu and saturating it with flavor. If they're too thickly cut, they'll retain some raw crunch.

Miso-Maple Tofu with Melted Onions

SERVES 3 OR 4

3 tablespoons olive oil
1 tablespoon plus 1 teaspoon maple syrup
1 tablespoon miso paste
½ teaspoon salt

1 small or ½ large white onion, sliced into
    thin strips (⅛ inch or less)
One 15-ounce block firm tofu,
    blotted dry and cut into 8 slabs

Preheat the oven to 375°F.

In a small bowl, whisk together the oil, maple syrup, miso paste, and salt. Spread the onions in a medium baking dish (one in which the tofu will fit in snugly in a single layer—an 8 x 8 inch or 7 x 11 inch works well). Add a spoonful of the marinade to the onions and mix to evenly coat, then arrange the tofu on top. Drizzle the remaining marinade over the tofu and coat it evenly using your hands.

Bake for 40 to 50 minutes, flipping once and stirring gently, until the tofu is nicely caramelized and the onions are "melty." Serve hot.

This dish always gets a lot of love when I serve it at dinner parties—I suppose the tangy and sweet flavors are a bit of a surprise, as they really concentrate over the course of forty minutes in the oven. As someone who loves pineapple juice, I often keep a few cans in my cupboard for cooking and drinking (the Trader Joe's brand is very good!). But you can easily substitute orange juice here. And feel free to increase or decrease the sriracha, depending on your personal threshold for spice.

Pineapple-Sriracha Tofu

SERVES 3 OR 4

¾ cup pineapple juice
2 tablespoons brown sugar
1 tablespoon olive oil
2 teaspoons sriracha
Zest and juice of 1 small lime

½ teaspoon salt
Freshly ground black pepper
One 15-ounce block firm tofu,
      blotted dry and cut into 8 slabs

Preheat the oven to 425°F.

In a cup or small bowl, whisk together the pineapple juice, brown sugar, olive oil, sriracha, lime zest and juice, salt, and several grinds of black pepper. Arrange the tofu in a baking dish—one in which it fits comfortably in a single layer (an 8 x 8 inch or 7 x 11 inch works well)—then pour the marinade over. Let marinate at least 20 minutes, or up to a few hours (in which case, hold off preheating the oven). Transfer to the oven and bake, flipping once halfway through, until the tofu is browned and the sauce is reduced, about 40 minutes. Serve hot.

Sweet balsamic vinegar and salty, umami-rich soy sauce geographically don't make sense together, but in dressings and marinades they are surprisingly compatible. Don't bother using your really nice balsamic—in this treatment, the cheaper stuff is just fine. And once baked off, this tofu is surprisingly versatile in sandwiches, salads, anywhere you might use a pre-seasoned block of store-bought tofu.

Balsamic—Soy Sauce Tofu

SERVES 3 OR 4

2 tablespoons balsamic vinegar
2 tablespoons soy sauce
2 tablespoons olive oil
1 teaspoon freshly ground black pepper

¾ teaspoon salt
One 15-ounce block firm tofu,
    blotted dry and cut into 8 slabs

Preheat the oven to 400°F.

In a cup or small bowl, whisk together the vinegar, soy sauce, olive oil, black pepper, and salt. Arrange the tofu pieces in a baking dish—one in which they fit in a snug single layer (an 8 x 8 inch or 7 x 11 inch works well)—then pour the marinade over the top, flipping the pieces to coat. Transfer to the oven and bake, flipping once halfway through, until the marinade is reduced and has caramelized somewhat on the tofu, about 30 minutes. Serve hot.

The tomato sauce in this tofu dish reduces to a thick, almost sticky consistency and is absolutely bursting with flavor. And the ginger doesn't get lost—it's got a good jolt of spice, rounded out with soy sauce and a touch of toasted sesame oil. Watch closely toward the end, as the saucy marinade can dry out in a flash. Leftovers make a great sandwich filling.

Tomato-Ginger Tofu

SERVES 3 OR 4

1 cup halved cherry tomatoes
2 tablespoons olive oil
1 tablespoon soy sauce
1 tablespoon grated ginger
2 cloves garlic, minced

½ teaspoon toasted sesame oil
¼ teaspoon salt
Freshly ground black pepper
One 15-ounce block firm tofu,
    blotted dry and cut into 8 slabs

Preheat the oven to 400°F.

Combine the tomatoes, olive oil, soy sauce, ginger, garlic, toasted sesame oil, salt, and several grinds of black pepper in a mini food processor or the cup that comes with an immersion blender and puree. Arrange the tofu in a baking dish—one in which it fits comfortably in a single layer (an 8 x 8 inch or 7 x 11 inch works well)—then pour the sauce over and turn the tofu pieces to coat. Bake, flipping the tofu once halfway through, until the sauce is thickened, 50 to 60 minutes. Serve hot.

Tofu scrambles are popular for a reason: They're a nutritionally dense, protein-packed, energizing breakfast. And since the leftovers reheat well, making a batch early in the week means quick midweek breakfasts later on (for best results, stir in the greens to order). This one forgoes the addition of turmeric that you'll find in many tofu scrambles (I'm convinced it's usually there just to make tofu curds look more like eggs, rather than for its flavor). Instead this scramble has a subtle maple kick, giving the dish the suggestion of having bumped elbows with some pancakes and syrup.

Breakfast Tofu Scramble

SERVES 4

One 15-ounce block firm tofu, blotted dry
Olive oil
1 cup diced winter squash or sweet potato
  (½-inch cubes)
4 scallions, green and white parts, sliced
½ teaspoon salt
1 tablespoon maple syrup
1½ teaspoons sriracha

2 teaspoons water
One 15-ounce can black beans,
  drained and rinsed
½ cup coarsely chopped fresh cilantro
4 handfuls tender greens,
  such as baby spinach or baby kale
Freshly ground black pepper
1 avocado, quartered

Slice the tofu into a few thick slabs, then lay them on a cutting board and use a fork to mash them into crumbles.

In a wide skillet, warm a splash of olive oil over medium heat. Add the squash or sweet potato and cook, stirring every now and then, until it starts to sear and caramelize. Test for doneness—if it's not fully cooked, add about 2 teaspoons water to the pan, cover (with a lid or baking sheet), and cook for a few minutes, allowing it to finish cooking by steam. Stir in the scallions, crumbled tofu, and salt. Cook for about 5 minutes, stirring often, until the pan is dry.

Clear a space in the middle of the skillet and add the maple syrup, sriracha, and water, letting it bubble away, then stir in the tofu and vegetables to coat. Add the beans and cook for 2 to 3 minutes, until heated through, then add the cilantro. If you're planning to set aside some of the scramble as leftovers, do that before adding the greens. Otherwise, add the greens and toss with the scramble until wilted. Season with black pepper.

Serve hot, with an avocado quarter per person.

This is a quick summer dish that capitalizes on juicy tomatoes and requires the stove to be turned on for just a few minutes. My favorite part is the contrast of temperatures—the warm, savory tomatoes over the cool, custardy tofu. You'll lose those temperature and texture contrasts if you swap in firm or extra-firm tofu, but spooning the tomatoes over slabs of grilled or pan-fried tofu is a worthwhile variation.

Silken Tofu with Soy-Sauced Tomatoes

SERVES 2 AS A MAIN, OR 4 AS A SIDE

1 cup (½ pint) cherry tomatoes, halved
1 tablespoon soy sauce
1 teaspoon olive oil
Freshly ground black pepper

1 block silken tofu, about 12 ounces, chilled
Toasted sesame oil
Thinly sliced scallions (optional)
Thinly sliced basil (optional)

In a small saucepan or skillet, combine the tomatoes, soy sauce, olive oil, and many grinds of black pepper. Place over low heat and cook for 5 to 7 minutes, just until the tomatoes start to soften and juices collect in the pan.

Carefully cut the tofu into 2 wide slabs (or 4 smaller ones) and place on plates or in shallow bowls. Divide the warm tomatoes on top. Add a judicious drizzle of toasted sesame oil, then sprinkle with scallions and basil, if using. Serve immediately.

I love a banh mi, the Vietnamese sandwich bursting with pickled vegetables, a protein of choice, and often some kind of pate and mayonnaise. But when making them at home, I usually take some liberties, as I do here. The particular baguette they're known for, first of all, can be a hassle to find even in New York City, so I opt for a ciabatta roll, which, with its crusty exterior and soft, airy interior, I think is the next best thing. And for the protein, I use either prepared baked tofu or a homemade marinated and baked one. And then the peanut-miso spread is certainly not pate, but it is sweet and savory, and adds some necessary richness.

Banh Mi-*Ish*

SERVES 4

Quick pickled veg
1 large carrot
1 medium cucumber
½ teaspoon salt

1 tablespoon rice vinegar or apple cider
vinegar

Peanut-miso spread
2 tablespoons natural peanut butter,
chunky or smooth
2 tablespoons miso paste

2 teaspoons maple syrup
2 to 4 teaspoons water

To assemble the sandwiches
4 sandwich rolls, such as ciabatta, split
1 recipe Balsamic–Soy Sauce Tofu
(page 42), Pineapple-Sriracha Tofu

(page 41), or store-bought baked and
marinated tofu
Large handful mint, basil, cilantro leaves,
or a combination

PICKLE THE VEGETABLES: Use a vegetable peeler to first peel the carrot and cucumber. Lay the carrot flat on a cutting board and carefully shave it into long, wide ribbons, again using the vegetable peeler. Do the same with the cucumber, shaving into the vegetable just until you get to the seeds. (Discard the seedy core.) Combine the vegetables with the salt in a small bowl and let stand to soften slightly for 5 to 10 minutes, then add the vinegar.

MAKE THE PEANUT-MISO SPREAD: Whisk together the peanut butter, miso paste, and maple syrup in a small bowl. Whisk in water a teaspoon or two at a time, just until the mixture softens a touch and looks glossy.

TO ASSEMBLE THE SANDWICHES: Toast the split rolls. Spread one side of each with a heaping tablespoon of the peanut-miso spread. Divide the tofu on top, followed by a pile of pickled vegetables and several whole herb leaves. Close up the sandwiches and serve.

The secret to crispy-fried tofu is to get the tofu really dry before you start frying. Here, it's wrapped in a clean towel, weighed down under a heavy object, and "pressed" for 15 to 30 minutes. Then it's fried in neutral oil until golden brown. Serving the crispy-fried tofu in a salad like this is by no means the only way—combine it with a prepared sauce and scoop over rice, or add it to a stir-fry with a medley of vegetables—but since it looks a bit like croutons, I've gone in the salad direction.

Charred Romaine Salad with Tofu "Croutons"

SERVES 4

One 15-ounce block firm tofu, blotted dry
Canola, grapeseed, or vegetable oil,
     for frying
Salt
1 tablespoon soy sauce
1 tablespoon balsamic vinegar
1 teaspoon honey or maple syrup
2 tablespoons olive oil

Freshly ground black pepper
2 romaine hearts, quartered lengthwise
1 avocado, cut into chunks
½ cup halved cherry tomatoes
1 small cucumber, cut into half- or
     quarter-inch rings
2 scallions, green and white parts,
     thinly sliced

Press the tofu: Slice the tofu into a few broad slabs, about 1 inch thick. Lay a clean kitchen towel over your work surface, then place the tofu slabs side-by-side at one end. Wrap the tofu up in the towel, folding it over and tucking the ends so that it's surrounded by a few layers, then place a heavy item—a cast-iron skillet or a baking dish—on top. Allow the tofu to compress and drain like this for at least 15 minutes, ideally 30.

Cut each tofu slab into 1-inch cubes. Warm about ¼ inch oil in a medium skillet over medium-high heat. When hot—test the temperature by dipping a piece of tofu into the oil; it should sizzle immediately—gently add the tofu. Fry until golden brown on all sides, carefully turning them as necessary, which will take 8 to 10 minutes on the first side, and then less on the others as the oil continues to heat up. Use a slotted spoon to transfer the cooked tofu to a paper towel to drain and sprinkle with salt.

In a small bowl or liquid measuring cup, whisk together the soy sauce, vinegar, honey or maple syrup, olive oil, and a few grinds of black pepper.

To char the romaine hearts, hold each quarter of romaine with metal tongs and place directly in the flame of a gas burner or beneath the flame of a broiler set to high. Char both cut sides of the romaine until lightly blackened. Coarsely chop them and transfer to a serving bowl.

Add the avocado, tomatoes, cucumber, scallions, and tofu to the salad bowl, and while warm, toss with the dressing to taste. It's best to serve this salad immediately, while the texture of the tofu is crisp on the outside and soft on the inside.

This dish is indisputably cute—parcels of tofu that have little pockets stuffed with spicy, salty ginger-scallion sauce. Each piece can serve as a traditional vegetarian main for the center of the plate, with a simple salad on the side. Make sure to grate the ginger on a Microplane or the equivalent, because chunks of ginger, even small ones, are a bit unpleasant here.

Ginger-Scallion Stuffed Tofu

SERVES 4

3 tablespoons plus 1 teaspoon olive oil, divided
1 bunch scallions, green and white parts, thinly sliced
2 tablespoons finely grated ginger
1 tablespoon minced garlic

½ teaspoon salt
1 teaspoon toasted sesame oil
½ teaspoon plus a pinch of sugar, divided
Freshly ground black pepper
One 15-ounce block firm tofu
2 tablespoons soy sauce

Warm 1½ tablespoons of the olive oil in a small saucepan or skillet over medium heat, then add the scallions, ginger, garlic, and salt. Cook just until softened and the raw bite has cooked off, 2 to 3 minutes. Remove from the heat and add 1½ tablespoons of the remaining olive oil, the sesame oil, the pinch of sugar, and several grinds of black pepper. Let cool until safe to handle.

Lay the tofu on a cutting board widthwise, like an envelope, and slice into 4 quarters. Use a clean towel to thoroughly blot them dry. Then hold each one in your hand and, using a small sharp knife, cut a pocket into each slab, taking care not to cut all the way through (though it's not the end of the world if you do). Repeat with remaining tofu pieces.

Preheat the oven to 375°F.

In a small bowl, stir together the soy sauce, the remaining 1 teaspoon olive oil, and the remaining ½ teaspoon sugar.

As best you can, gently tuck a heaping teaspoon of the ginger-scallion mixture into the pockets of each piece of tofu, mounding it over the top of the tofu. (Alternatively, slice each piece of tofu in half horizontally, like a layer cake, and sandwich the ginger-scallion mixture in between.) Arrange in a single layer in a small baking dish. Drizzle the soy sauce mixture over the top.

Transfer to the oven and bake for 30 minutes, spooning some of the soy sauce mixture over the tops as they cook. Turn them upright on plates or a serving platter, top with any ginger-scallion sauce left in the baking dish, and serve hot.

CHAPTER 6

Essential Hearty Greens

A few big bunches of greens are never not in my shopping basket and in my refrigerator. A meal just doesn't feel complete without them. This is because every nutritionist you talk to will encourage loading up on greens—surely there's a point at which you can overdo it, but that's likely a ways in the distance for most of us—and also because there are so many delicious ways to enjoy them.

When I refer to hearty greens, I mean the vitamin-, mineral-, and fiber-rich, sturdy dark green ones: kale, chard, mustard greens, beet greens, mature spinach (not the baby leaves). Their textures and flavors vary from green to green—spinach and chard are both soft and sweet; kale has an earthy, virtuous-tasting bitterness; mustard greens and mature arugula can offer a nasal tract–cleaning burn—and they're all most flavorful in their raw state. But when they're cooked, they become much milder, lending themselves to interchangeable use. Each one has a different cooking time. When you're combining them for recipes like Marinated Greens (page 54), you can (and should!) use any combination of greens, but cook each one separately.

And I'm no stranger to pre-bagged, pre-chopped kale and other greens—I use them often in cooked preparations like sautés and soups. The great appeal of these bagged greens for me is not having to wash them at home, a tedious but necessary task. But the bagged hearty greens—kale is the most widely available of them—often contain a fair amount of stem. So you won't want to use those in raw treatments, such as the salads that appear on pages 66 to 71.

A good salad spinner can be your savior when you wash your kale, chard, and any other greens. One that does not drain out the bottom is most ideal—this way the bowl of the salad spinner functions as a basin for the greens. Cover the greens with plenty of water in the salad spinner bowl and vigorously swish the dirty greens in the water to loosen any grit. Then lift the greens from the water and transfer them to the accompanying basket to drain. Pour out the dirty water—if you see a fair amount of dirt and debris in it, repeat this process once or twice. Once the water runs clean, spin the greens dry.

Another thing to keep in mind when you pick up a bunch of greens at the grocery store is that their weight can vary drastically. A bunch of kale might weigh 4 ounces, or it might weigh 14 ounces. This is because retailers purchase vegetables like kale by the pallet or crate, and the price varies greatly throughout the year. To maintain consistent pricing retailers try to get more bunches from the crate when the price is high; when it's cheap, they divide it into fewer, larger bunches. My recipes call for a "large" bunch, which means somewhere in the 10- to 12-ounce range. Use the scale at your grocery store so that you know what you're working with.

These recipes put the focus directly on the greens, with easy ways to turn marinated greens into meals, three "keeper" raw green salads, as well as a hearty and warming ribollita and some fun snacks. But be sure to look elsewhere in the book for more recipes—there's no way greens can be completely contained to just one chapter!

Pre-cooking greens is a terrific way to extend their shelf life—once they're cooked, they'll be edible for up to a week, which is several days more than what you typically get from raw greens. It's also a way to frontload the labor of cleaning and cooking them so that they can be more easily put to use in omelets, sandwiches, pasta, and more. And marinating them—that is, seasoning them—gets you that much closer to a tasty meal when dinnertime rolls around. I prefer to use a variety of greens here, but if you only have one type on hand, don't sweat it. And for a neutral flavor profile, leave out the garlic, pepper flakes, and lemon, and season only with olive oil, salt, and pepper.

Marinated Greens

SERVES 4

2 bunches (about 1½ pounds) leafy greens: Swiss chard, kale, mature spinach, beet greens, or a combination of any of the above, washed
2 tablespoons olive oil, divided

1 clove garlic, minced
Pinch red pepper flakes, or to taste
Salt
Fresh lemon juice

Trim off and discard the tough stems from the greens. Heat 1 tablespoon of the olive oil in a wide skillet or saucepan over medium-low heat. Add the garlic and red pepper flakes and stir for about 1 minute, until fragrant. Pile in the greens, in batches if necessary, and add a splash of water (you can also cover with a lid to compress them). Add a big pinch of salt and gently cook, stirring with tongs, until wilted and tender. Cooking times will vary depending on type of green, so watch and taste as you go. If cooking a combination of different greens, cook each type separately. Add a splash of water to the pan if it dries out.

Transfer to a colander to drain and cool until safe to handle. Gently squeeze out excess liquid using your hands or a spatula or wooden spoon, pressing against the side of the colander. Coarsely chop the greens, then transfer them to a medium bowl and toss with the remaining 1 tablespoon olive oil and a few drops of lemon juice. Taste and add more lemon juice, red pepper flakes, or salt as needed. Store in an airtight container in the refrigerator; allow to come to room temperature before serving.

Ribollita is one of those "rustic" dishes that's survived through the centuries because its combination of everyday ingredients completely surpasses the sum of its parts. Beans, vegetables, loads of kale, and stale bread become the kind of stew you can eat with a fork. Cabbage, Swiss chard, or collards can be subbed for some or all of the kale, but try to use an Italian-style or other rustic type of bread that's not too dense and contains just flour and water—no fat or eggs. Leftovers are a thing to celebrate, as this stew improves in flavor as it sits.

Ribollita

SERVES 4 TO 6

½ pound (1 cup) dried white beans
    (cannellini, navy, or great northern),
    soaked overnight in plenty of water
Olive oil
Salt
1 large white or yellow onion, chopped
2 medium carrots, chopped
3 stalks celery, chopped
4 cloves garlic, sliced
¼ teaspoon red pepper flakes

2 bay leaves
½ teaspoon dried thyme
One 28-ounce can whole tomatoes,
    drained
1 pound (2 big bunches) kale, stemmed and
    chopped into bite-size pieces,
    or equivalent bagged chopped kale
4 or 5 thick slices Italian bread
    (4 to 6 ounces), torn into pieces

Place the soaked beans in a medium saucepan and cover with water by an inch. Bring to a boil, then reduce to a gentle simmer and add 1 tablespoon olive oil and 1 heaping teaspoon salt. Simmer until the beans are tender—start checking after 30 minutes, but be patient, allowing as much time as necessary until there's no trace of grainy, uncooked bean left. Season with additional salt to taste—the broth should be flavorful—and add more water to the pan to keep the beans just submerged. Remove from the heat and use a potato masher or spoon to coarsely mash some of the beans and thicken the liquid a bit. This step can be done a day ahead.

In a soup pot or Dutch oven, warm 3 tablespoons olive oil over medium heat. Add the onion, carrots, celery, garlic, red pepper flakes, bay leaves, and thyme and cook, stirring often, until the vegetables are tender but not browned, 15 to 20 minutes. Add the tomatoes one by one, carefully crushing them with your hand as you add them to the pot, followed by the beans and their cooking liquid and the kale. The soup should be pretty thick, but if it's stiff, add a few splashes of water to loosen it up. Bring to a boil, then lower the heat and simmer for 20 minutes. Stir in the bread and cook for 10 to 12 minutes more, until the bread breaks down and thickens the soup. Taste for seasoning.

Ladle the hot soup into bowls and drizzle each serving with a glug of olive oil.

This is a simple appetizer that's a hit every time I serve it, due in large part to the vast appeal of warm cheesy things. You can assemble the toasts in advance, up to the point of spreading the toast with goat cheese. Then when it's time to serve, just pop the toasts under the broiler to heat them up, and then top with the greens. A spreadable vegan cheese works well, too, though in that case I find it best to skip the broiling step.

Broiled Goat Cheese Toasts with Marinated Greens

MAKES 12 SMALL TOASTS

12 slices of baguette about ¾ inch thick, or other bread cut into 10 bite-size pieces
Olive oil
½ cup soft goat cheese

1 cup Marinated Greens (page 54), at room temperature
Zest of 1 lemon
Flaky salt
Freshly ground black pepper

Preheat the broiler to high.

Arrange the toasts on a baking sheet and brush both sides with olive oil. Transfer to the broiler and broil for 2 to 4 minutes, until lightly golden on the top. Flip the toasts. Smear each slice with about 2 teaspoons goat cheese, drizzle with a bit of olive oil, and return to the broiler. Broil, watching carefully, for just a minute or two, to heat through and lightly brown. Transfer to a serving platter and divide the greens on top. Zest the lemon over everything, sprinkle with a bit of flaky salt and black pepper, add a drizzle of olive oil, and serve while the toasts are still warm.

These simple tostadas can be gussied up in all kinds of ways—Roasted, Mashed Butternut Squash (page 16) makes an excellent topping, too, as do Roasted Mushrooms (page 136), the mashed zucchini dip sans almonds (page 217), or a fried egg as embellishment. But the beauty of a tostada is its simplicity, allowing the toppings to shine with the help of a few zingy garnishes and a giant, crispy disc of a baked or fried tortilla. The soft texture and concentrated flavor of the greens is prominent here.

Black Bean Tostadas with Marinated Greens

MAKES 6 TOSTADAS

6 small corn or flour tortillas
Olive oil
Salt
1 small red or white onion, sliced into very
    thin strips
1 to 2 tablespoons apple cider vinegar

One 15-ounce can black beans, drained
    and rinsed
1 cup Marinated Greens (page 54)
Crumbled cotija or feta cheese
Thinly sliced serrano or jalapeño chile
Lime wedges, for serving
Salsa or hot sauce, for serving

Preheat the oven to 375°F.

Brush both sides of the tortillas with olive oil, then arrange on a baking sheet in a single layer (though it's fine if they overlap a bit) and sprinkle with salt. Bake until crisp, about 20 minutes, flipping halfway.

Pickle the onion: Combine the onion with a few pinches of salt in a small bowl and mix with your hands until softened and glistening. Cover with a tablespoon or two of vinegar and set aside.

Place the beans in a small saucepan and set over medium-low heat. Add a few splashes of water and mash with a spoon, adding more water as needed, until you've got a spreadable consistency. Season with salt.

Spread the beans over the crisped tortillas, then divide the greens over them. Top with pickled onion, cheese, and chile, and serve with lime wedges and salsa or hot sauce of choice.

Roasted scallions add a jolt of dare-I-say meaty flavor in these twice-baked potatoes, serving as something of a vegetarian substitute for the bacon bits that were in the ones I grew up eating. They're also less of a dairy bomb but make no compromises in terms of being rich and irresistible. Leave out the ricotta to make them vegan, but you may need to add a bit more milk to moisten the filling. The potatoes can be prepared well in advance, and even after being assembled and baked they freeze well packed in an airtight container or resealable bag.

Twice-Baked Potatoes with Marinated Greens and Roasted Scallions

MAKES 8 TWICE-BAKED POTATOES

1 bunch scallions, ends trimmed
Olive oil
4 medium russet potatoes, about
    1½ pounds, scrubbed and blotted dry
Salt
1 cup Marinated Greens (page 54),
    coarsely chopped
1 clove garlic, minced

½ cup whole or unsweetened nondairy
    milk, plus more as needed
½ cup fresh ricotta cheese
2 swipes lemon zest
¼ cup parsley, mint, or basil leaves, or a
    combination
6 Castelvetrano olives, pitted
3 tablespoons coarsely chopped toasted
    almonds, hazelnuts, or walnuts

Preheat the oven to 425°F.

Place the scallions on one side of a baking sheet and rub them with a bit of olive oil. Rub the potatoes with olive oil, too, and sprinkle all over with salt, then arrange on the other end of the baking sheet. Transfer to the oven. Bake for 10 to 15 minutes, until the scallions are wilted, golden brown in parts, and beginning to crisp. Remove them from the baking sheet and set aside on a plate to cool. Return the pan to the oven and bake the potatoes for another 45 minutes or so, until tender. Cool until safe to handle. (If not proceeding immediately with the recipe, turn off the oven.)

Cut the potatoes in half lengthwise and scoop out most of the flesh, but leaving enough behind so that the remaining skins can function as vessels. Return the skins to the baking sheet.

In a medium bowl, mash and then whip the potatoes until smooth and few lumps remain. Coarsely chop the scallions and add to the potatoes along with the greens, garlic, milk, ricotta, and a swipe of lemon zest. Stir with a spatula, adding a bit more milk as needed to achieve a consistency that's creamy but not loose. Divide the filling among the potato skins. Transfer to the oven and bake the potatoes for 15 minutes, or until lightly browned and heated through.

Mince together the herbs, olives, nuts, and the remaining swipe of lemon zest with a big pinch of salt on a cutting board until finely chopped. Scrape the mixture into a small bowl, stir in about 2 tablespoons olive oil, and taste for seasoning. Spoon a teaspoon or so of the mixture over each potato half just before serving.

The success of carbonara, in my experience, is literally that flick of the wrist: As you add eggs to the hot noodles, you must *move* the noodles, so as to ensure there's no time for the egg to rest on a still, hot surface and curdle. And as with all pasta dishes, it's crucial to properly season the pasta cooking water—or the finished dish will taste flat. Season it, as they say, to taste like the sea. This carbonara, which is the evolution of a recipe I've been making for a long time, uses fried capers to bring the oomph of flavor—a component I first discovered years ago on Heidi Swanson's 101 Cookbooks blog.

Carbonara with Marinated Greens and Fried Capers

SERVES 3 OR 4

2 tablespoons capers, drained if in brine,
    rinsed if packed in salt
Olive oil
1 whole egg plus 1 egg yolk
Salt
8 ounces spaghetti

⅔ cup Marinated Greens (page 54)
Freshly grated Parmesan cheese
Freshly ground black pepper
Fried breadcrumbs (page 182; optional)
Minced parsley or chives (optional)

Place the capers on a few layers of paper towel and gently blot as thoroughly dry as you can. Place a small skillet over medium heat and warm a splash of olive oil. Add the capers and cook, swirling the pan every now and then, until they crisp and begin to unfurl, 1 to 2 minutes. (Watch out for sputtering oil.) Transfer them to a paper towel–lined plate to drain.

Crack the egg and yolk into a small bowl. Add ¼ teaspoon salt and whisk to combine.

Meanwhile, bring a pot of water to a boil and salt it well. Add the spaghetti and cook until just tender, using the package instructions as a guide. Reserve a few ladlesful of the cooking water, then drain, and return the noodles to the pot.

Whisk a few tablespoons of the hot pasta cooking water into the eggs to temper them a bit, then slowly pour in the pasta, stirring constantly with tongs or a wooden spoon as you do so. The eggs will cook as they make contact with the noodles, creating a sauce. Stir in the marinated greens. Add a ladleful of the pasta cooking water as needed to loosen the noodles—the pasta should be appealingly creamy but not wet.

Transfer to warm plates or bowls, garnish with the capers, cheese, plenty of black pepper, and breadcrumbs and herbs, if using. Serve immediately.

This may sound like a strange combination if your first association with "peanut butter" is "jelly"—but focus on the peanut's savory side, and it makes perfect sense (if you avoid eating peanuts, almond butter makes an excellent substitute). I like this sandwich best with a soft wheat bread and when the marinated greens have some bitterness. The scallion cuts the richness of the peanut butter just a bit, but if you don't like raw allium, omit it.

Peanut Butter and Greens Sandwich

MAKES 1 SANDWICH

2 slices sandwich bread
3 tablespoons natural peanut butter
Salt, if needed
¼ cup Marinated Greens (page 54)
1 scallion, lights green and white parts,
    thinly sliced

Fresh lemon juice
Sriracha
Olive oil or butter
Flaky salt

Spread both sides of the bread with peanut butter and, depending on the saltiness of the peanut butter, sprinkle with salt to taste. Spread the marinated greens over one slice and top with the scallion, a squeeze of lemon juice, and sriracha to taste. Close the sandwich.

Place a skillet over medium heat. When hot, pour in a thin film of olive oil or melt a pat of butter in it. Place the sandwich top-side down and cook until golden brown, about 3 minutes, pressing down gently if needed so that it begins to brown. Add a bit more olive oil or butter if the pan looks dry, then flip and repeat. Sprinkle the sandwich with a pinch of flaky salt, slice in half, and serve immediately.

SALT YOUR SANDWICH

Adding a pinch of flaky finishing salt to the top of your sandwich isn't the most intuitive thing to do—especially since the seared bread already has some crunch. But I've been doing this ever since I saw it done at a cafe for a grilled cheese sandwich I ordered. The little savory, brittle bursts are totally delectable and have a way of elevating the sandwich into something special.

The color and papery texture of roasted seaweed snacks, which are miraculously dense with nutrients despite being lighter than a feather, have always reminded me of kale chips—and this easy snack combines the two. Toasted sesame oil adds a lick of richness, and then if you've got it on hand or care to seek it out, seasoning the chips with shichimi tōgarashi, the seven-spice blend (that includes dried chiles, pepper, sesame seeds, and citrus peel) that's often at the table in little vials at ramen restaurants, takes them in an exciting direction.

Kale and Nori Chips

MAKES ABOUT 8 CUPS

1 bunch Tuscan kale (about 12 ounces), stemmed and torn into small pieces
1 snack package (.375 ounces/10 grams) roasted seaweed snacks

2 tablespoons olive oil
1½ teaspoons toasted sesame oil
Shichimi tōgarashi (optional)
Salt

Preheat the oven to 325°F.

Make sure the kale is thoroughly dry, or it won't crisp very well.

In a large bowl, toss the kale and seaweed snacks with the oils using your hands, making sure everything is evenly coated. Divide between two baking sheets and transfer to the oven. Bake for 10 minutes, then stir and rotate the pans. Return to the oven and bake for another 5 to 10 minutes, until the kale is crisp. Sprinkle the shichimi tōgarashi liberally over everything while still warm, if using, then season carefully with salt—a little goes a long way. Allow to cool. Packed in an airtight container, these will keep for up to 5 days.

Three Hearty Green Salads

Kale salads may not be as stylish as they once were, but I still find them appealing for lots of reasons: they keep well, they're hearty, and they deliver a dose of nutrients. And when they're good, they're *really good*. In the cooler months, when fresh salad greens aren't as widely available or at least aren't as good, these hearty green salads come right to the rescue.

KALE SALAD WITH ROASTED SQUASH AND FENNEL

SERVES 4

The dressing—a mix of maple syrup, lemon juice, and olive oil, plus an optional jolt of ginger—could make anything taste good, and the salad, with its autumnal profile, works just as well in holiday menus as it does in packed weekday lunches. My friend Lesley Enston, a very skilled cook whom I've shared many a delicious home-cooked meal with, substitutes honey for the maple, and it's equally stellar. Add some crumbled feta if you'd like a tangy, creamy element.

2 cups winter squash cut into bite-size pieces (butternut, kabocha, or acorn)

3 tablespoons olive oil, divided

Salt

Freshly ground black pepper

2 tablespoons fresh lemon juice

1 to 1½ tablespoons maple syrup or honey

2 teaspoons finely grated ginger (optional)

1 small or ½ large bulb fennel, cored

1 large bunch kale (about 12 ounces), stemmed and torn into bite-size pieces

¼ cup crumbled feta cheese (optional)

Preheat the oven to 425°F.

Spread the squash on a baking sheet, then toss with 1½ tablespoons of the olive oil and sprinkle with a big pinch of salt and several grinds of black pepper. Roast until tender, 15 to 20 minutes, stirring once or twice. Cool.

Whisk together the remaining 1½ tablespoons olive oil, the lemon juice, maple syrup or honey, and ginger, if using, in a serving bowl. Cut the fennel into thinnest-possible shavings, preferably using a mandoline or, if not, a very sharp knife. Add the fennel and squash to the bowl with the dressing and stir to coat. Let stand for about 5 minutes, which will soften up the fennel, then add the kale and toss to coat with your hands. Top with the cheese, if using.

KALE SALAD WITH ROASTED
SQUASH AND FENNEL,
PAGE 67

KALE OR CHARD WITH OLIVE
VINAIGRETTE AND CRISP
BREADCRUMBS,
PAGE 70

GARLIC-SESAME KALE
AND AVOCADO SALAD,
PAGE 70

GARLIC-SESAME KALE AND AVOCADO SALAD

SERVES 4

At a dinner party a few years ago, I ate a stupid-simple salad that wowed me: using her hands, the host mashed together a bunch of torn kale with a ripe avocado; there was some salt and pepper, but otherwise, that's it. It was so good, cool and creamy and substantial. I later found several iterations of it online, including on my friends' Beau Ciolino and Matt Armato's fun blog, Probably This. Use an avocado that's ripe—one that'd be good for guacamole—because a rock-hard, underripe one won't break down.

1 small clove garlic, peeled

½ teaspoon salt

½ teaspoon ground cumin

Juice of ½ lemon

1 ripe avocado, cubed

1 large bunch kale (about 12 ounces), stemmed and torn into bite-size pieces

2 tablespoons toasted sesame seeds

Place the garlic clove on a cutting board, smash with the side of your knife, and sprinkle with salt. Mince and mash, flattening the garlic out over the cutting board using the side of the knife, until you have garlic paste.

Place the avocado in a salad bowl and add the garlic paste, cumin, and lemon juice. Pile the kale on top, then use your hands to "massage" the kale and avocado together, until the kale is well coated, collapsed slightly, and the avocado is mashed among all the leaves. Sprinkle the seeds over the top, toss, and serve—within an hour of assembling, as the avocado will, unfortunately, oxidize.

KALE OR CHARD WITH OLIVE VINAIGRETTE AND CRISP BREADCRUMBS

SERVES 4

Alexandra Stafford, author of *Bread, Toast, Crumbs* and the blog Alexandra Cooks, deserves a Nobel Prize for championing breadcrumbs as she does: They constitute a whole chapter in her book! In this salad, inspired by a Swiss chard salad she shared on her blog, they're as much a lead ingredient as the greens, lending crispiness and a bit of body to the otherwise-uniform-in-texture greens. The olive-forward vinaigrette is delicious on romaine and butter-leaf salads as well.

2 slices good, fresh artisan bread

Olive oil

Salt

1 large bunch kale (about 12 ounces) or Swiss chard, stemmed

1 small clove garlic, peeled

Pinch salt

8 green olives, preferably Castelvetrano, pitted

1 lemon

2 tablespoons plain yogurt

Pinch red pepper flakes

Tear the bread into small pieces and pulse them in a mini food processor, or use your hands to break the bread into irregularly sized bread crumbs. The largest should be about the size of a peanut, and you should have about 1 cup crumbs. (I don't trim off the crusts.) Warm a film of olive oil in a medium skillet over medium-low heat, and when hot, add the bread. Cook, stirring frequently, until golden brown and crisp, 5 to 7 minutes. Transfer to a plate and season with salt.

Roll the greens into cigar shapes and chiffonade them: slice into thin wisps. Pile into a serving bowl.

Place the garlic and salt in a mortar and pound it with a pestle to a paste. Add the olives and pound to a paste. Zest the lemon into the olives, then add the juice from half the lemon. Stir in the yogurt, 3 tablespoons olive oil, and several grinds of black pepper, then taste for seasoning.

Toss most of the dressing over the greens, followed by the breadcrumbs. Add more dressing to taste. Serve within an hour or so, before the crisp breadcrumbs become soggy.

If you don't have a mortar and pestle, use a mini food processor to pulverize the garlic and olives, or chop them finely by hand, then stir them into the remaining dressing ingredients.

CHAPTER 7

Beans, Canned and Dried

Given their ubiquity—is there a cuisine in which they don't appear?—it's easy to take beans for granted, to forget how special they are. But beans are a miracle food if there ever was one. Nutritionists and other health professionals consistently reiterate this: Beans are an excellent source of plant-based protein, which vegans and vegetarians have long known, but they're also loaded with fiber (few of us eat enough fiber), complex carbs, and a good dose of vitamins and minerals. All this in a little bean!

We're also lucky they're so affordable and so plentifully available. I always have a few cans of beans in my cupboard, and because in my adulthood I've become something of a bean nut, I belong to a bean club, a coveted (for folks like me) offering from the celebrated heirloom bean mavens at Rancho Gordo, where a few times a year I get a box full of delicious dried beans. For me, this means that with beans on hand, I always have the building blocks of a nutritious and satisfying meal.

That said, it's pretty rare that beans generate excitement in cooks and eaters. I hope to remedy that. To start, there's the glory that is a simmering pot of home-cooked beans. These aren't quick, but they are easy, and if you haven't cooked beans yourself before, I urge you to give it a try. Like all cooking, the process of simmering beans pulls you into the present with its sensory immediacy, but beans are tethered to a primal lineage—I always feel connected to the cooks who precede me when I cook beans. Compared to canned beans, they have a more distinct and pleasant texture, as well as a savory and rich bean broth—an ingredient not to waste, but also something to enrich a great many dishes (and even to sip on).

But canned beans spare us the soaking and simmering, and are therefore tremendously useful. Also, because they're pressure cooked in their cans, some people who have issues digesting beans are fine with them. I've included a selection of bean salads that aim to freshen up this genre of potluck food, taking them in smoky, or citrusy, or summery directions. And in most recipes, it's fine to use canned beans instead of home-cooked beans. The exception are those recipes in which the whole pot of beans—beans, broth, and all—is used in its entirety in the dish, such as in my Ancho Bean Chili (page 84) or the Baked White Beans with Chicories (page 77). In these cases, you'll want to block out the necessary time to cook your beans from scratch. But with proper appreciation and the right mind-set, I think you'll enjoy it.

A last note: While the color of a bean will affect the look of a finished dish (and its broth—black beans create an inky broth), I find that the flavors of different types of beans aren't nearly as pronounced as their textures. In some cases you want something a bit sturdy, like pintos or black beans. Other times you want something ultra-creamy, like a cannellini or other white bean, and then there are times when a super-starchy texture is what's desired, as with kidney and lima beans. Consider the finished texture as you decide what type of bean to use in your cooking.

The real secret ingredient for home-cooked beans is liberally applied patience. You don't want undercooked beans, which are bad to eat and even worse to digest. Yet despite their timeless simplicity, cooking them causes a lot of confusion for many people. A few quick key points that will help you cook a perfect pot of beans with ease.

ON SOAKING: Soaking beans overnight in plenty of water can both speed up the cooking and draw out some of the *oligosaccharides*, the carbohydrates that our guts can't digest and therefore cause flatulence. But if you didn't have the foresight, skip soaking—just understand that the beans will take a bit longer to cook.

ON SALTING: There's a widespread belief that salting beans early in the cooking process causes the skins to toughen, but it's been disproven. Some cooks, like Samin Nosrat in *Salt, Fat, Acid, Heat,* even advocate soaking the beans in a salty brine prior to cooking them. I just start salting right when the water comes to a boil, and continue to taste and salt as they cook to ensure the beans are seasoned all the way through. Know that without salt, beans don't taste like much, so salt generously not just to make them taste good, but to taste like beans.

ON FAT: I always add a few good-size glugs of olive oil to the pot. This enriches the broth and gets absorbed into the beans and flavors them. When I want a pot of beans to be showy and worthy of a dinner party, I let the olive oil flow extra freely, adding it at various stages of the cooking, and then drizzle it over the beans to finish. This is the vegetarian cooking hack equivalent of throwing a fatty ham hock into the pot.

ON BEAN BROTH: Think of it as a twofer for home-cooked beans. Showcase bean broth by serving tender beans in a puddle of it, or use it as stock in soup or chili. Or a few ladlefuls can work as a flavorful thickening liquid when you're cooking something like a vegetable or bean ragout or, say, refried beans.

Put a pot of beans on the stove when you get home and let them cook when you unwind and prepare dinner, or when you've got some downtime over the weekend. Packed up in airtight containers, they'll provide handy nourishment through the week.

Brothy Beans

MAKES ABOUT 6 CUPS OF BEANS WITH BROTH

1 pound dried beans, soaked overnight (or not)

1 tablespoon salt, plus more to taste
¼ cup olive oil

Place the beans in a large pot and cover with about 2 inches of water. Put over high heat and bring to a boil. Add the salt and olive oil and reduce the heat to maintain a gentle simmer. Cook, stirring every now and then and skimming off any foam that gathers on the surface. Start checking for doneness after 30 minutes—either by tasting a bean or by cutting it in half. If the beans start to poke above the surface, add more water to keep them submerged—there should be enough liquid for the beans to be covered, but not swimming around. As you taste, also check for seasoning, adding more salt as needed. Before removing from the heat, make sure to taste several beans, all of which should be thoroughly tender. To store, let cool, then transfer—both the beans and their cooking liquid—to airtight containers and keep in the fridge for 3 to 5 days.

This is practically a one-stop meal—it needs no other accompaniment except maybe a few slices of garlic-rubbed toast on the side. I prefer the smaller, firmer lentils like Puy and beluga lentils to the standard brown or green ones in this dish because they retain their shape and some firmness, but either will work. But if you opt for standard brown and green lentils, be aware that they typically cook more quickly.

Lentil Skillet Bake with Spinach, Tomatoes, and Eggs

SERVES 4

1 cup lentils
1 teaspoon salt, divided
3 tablespoons olive oil
1 onion, thinly sliced
2 cloves garlic, sliced
¼ teaspoon dried thyme

Pinch red pepper flakes
1 tablespoon tomato paste
5 ounces baby spinach
1 cup halved cherry tomatoes
Freshly ground black pepper
4 eggs

In a medium saucepan, combine the lentils with 2 cups water and ½ teaspoon of the salt. Place over high heat and bring to a boil, then reduce to a simmer, cover, and cook for 15 to 20 minutes, until tender. Do not drain.

Preheat the oven to 375°F.

While the lentils cook, warm the olive oil in a large skillet over medium heat, then add the onion, garlic, thyme, and red pepper flakes. Cook for 4 to 5 minutes without disturbing to allow the onions to begin to caramelize, then stir and repeat until the onions are collapsed, blistered in places, and somewhat caramelized, about 20 minutes total. (This method is a bit of a caramelized onion hack—it's not the traditional low-and-slow method that yields melted, sweet, sticky onions, but it works well for weeknight cooking.) Stir in the tomato paste, then add the spinach and stir for 2 to 3 minutes, until wilted. Remove from the heat.

Add the tomatoes, the remaining ½ teaspoon salt, and the cooked lentils plus any liquid in the saucepan to the skillet. Add plenty of black pepper and taste for seasoning. Use a ladle or large spoon to make 4 divots in the lentils and crack an egg into each one. Transfer to the oven and cook for 15 to 20 minutes, until the whites are set and the yolks cooked to your liking. Serve hot.

Chicories, which include endive, radicchio, and escarole, are one of my favorite families of vegetables. They make a crunchy and refreshing wintertime salad, especially when in the Northeast, where I live, the options for local greens are sad and slim in the cold months. In this braise, they're cooked with beans and aromatic vegetables using the low-and-slow treatment, which transforms their bitter crunch into a sweet, sophisticated flavor that infuses the whole pot. It's classic comfort food: cheap, nutritious, hearty, and warming. It makes a lot—and leftovers are gold—but for me this is excellent vegan dinner party fare, served from bowls or ladled over thick slices of good artisan bread, with a simple salad on the side.

Baked White Beans with Chicories

MAKES 4 QUARTS, ENOUGH TO SERVE 8 TO 10

Olive oil

1 medium onion, or 2 fennel bulbs, cored and diced

2 medium carrots, diced

3 stalks celery, diced

5 cloves garlic, sliced

Salt

1 cup white wine

2 endives, sliced into ½-inch segments

1 medium radicchio, cored and cubed

1 recipe Brothy Beans (page 74) using white beans, such as cannellini, navy, or cassoulet

½ cup minced parsley, chives, fennel fronds, or a combination

Preheat the oven to 375°F.

Heat 3 tablespoons olive oil in a Dutch oven or other large oven-safe dish over medium heat. Add the onion or fennel, carrots, celery, garlic, and ¾ teaspoon salt. Cook, stirring every now and then, until reduced and beginning to caramelize, about 25 minutes. Pour in the wine and let it cook down for a few minutes, then add the endive and radicchio and cook until softened, 3 to 4 minutes. Use a slotted spoon to add the beans, then pour in enough of the broth to just cover the contents of the pot. If you need additional liquid, add water—you want everything *just* submerged. Bring to a boil, taste the broth and add a little salt if needed, then cover and transfer to the oven.

Cook for 1 hour. Remove the lid and cook for 20 to 30 minutes more, until the liquid is slightly reduced. Cool slightly, during which time the liquid will thicken a bit. Stir in the parsley or other herbs just before serving, while hot.

Here's a simple but decadent main, where a pool of soft, freshly cooked polenta is the vessel for savory, brothy beans and wilted greens. The spiciness comes by way of store-bought harissa, the Tunisian chile paste that's sometimes sold in a super-handy aluminum tube (the one made by Entube is my favorite). I find harissa to be such a great back-pocket ingredient, especially for simple dishes like this that welcome an assertive flavor direction. For the beans: "meaty" beans like gigante beans or big limas make an impression, as do any jewel-like heirloom bean you might be saving for a special occasion. Omitting the Parmesan garnish makes this an easy option for vegan guests.

Spicy Beans and Greens over Polenta

SERVES 4

1 cup polenta
½ teaspoon salt, plus more to taste
2 tablespoons olive oil, plus more
    for cooking
2 teaspoons harissa
3 cloves garlic, sliced

5 ounces spinach, baby kale, or
    stemmed Swiss chard, chopped
    into bite-sized pieces
2 cups Brothy Beans (page 74)
Grated Parmesan cheese (optional)
Freshly ground black pepper

Prepare the polenta: In a medium saucepan, bring 4 cups water to a boil, then reduce to a simmer and add the salt. While whisking, sprinkle in the polenta and keep whisking until the polenta incorporates into the liquid (rather than sinks to the bottom), 2 to 3 minutes. Reduce the heat to the lowest setting and simmer uncovered, whisking periodically to prevent the bottom from scorching, until the polenta is thick and the grains are tender, 15 to 20 minutes. Make sure to taste as you go, but use caution—it's very, very hot right out of the pot. Whisk in the olive oil.

Meanwhile, warm a splash of olive oil in a medium skillet over medium-low heat. Stir in the harissa and garlic. Cook until the garlic begins to soften, just about a minute, then add the greens and cook until wilted. Pour off any liquid in the pan and transfer the greens to a plate. Add the beans and their broth to the skillet and heat through, bringing the liquid to a simmer. Just before you're ready to serve, stir in the wilted greens.

Divide the polenta among 4 shallow serving bowls and spoon the beans over the top. Top each serving with cheese, if desired, and serve, passing the pepper at the table.

With home-cooked beans on hand in the refrigerator, this fueling and variable type of breakfast comes together very quickly. It utilizes the beans and the broth: Rather than using a slotted spoon to scoop out the beans, use a ladle, so as to collect the broth along with the beans. Substitute onion for the scallion, and incorporate all manner of leftover vegetables to embellish or replace: Wilted greens or Marinated Greens (page 54), Roasted Mushrooms (page 136), or a few spoonfuls of Roasted, Mashed Butternut Squash (page 16) stirred in.

Breakfast Beans

SERVES 1

1 cup Brothy Beans (page 74),
    including broth
Olive oil
3 or 4 scallions, green and white parts,
    sliced in half lengthwise
1 egg

½ avocado, cut into chunks
Hot sauce, for garnish
Sour cream or plain yogurt,
    for garnish (optional)
Toast or a griddled tortilla,
    for serving (optional)

In a small saucepan, heat the beans and broth over low heat until simmering and warmed all the way through (alternatively, warm the beans in the microwave in a microwave-safe bowl). Taste the broth and beans for seasoning.

Meanwhile, warm a splash of oil in a small skillet over medium-high heat. Add the scallions, arranging them in a single layer, and press down on them until they take on color and begin to soften, about 2 minutes. Flip and repeat, then transfer to a plate or cutting board, and, when safe to handle, coarsely chop. Add another splash of oil to the pan and fry the egg to desired doneness.

Place the egg over the beans. Add the avocado and scallions, then garnish with hot sauce and sour cream or yogurt, if using. Serve immediately, with the toast or tortilla, if you'd like.

Here's a simple lunch or dinner, requiring only a bit of patience, because caramelized alliums—onions, leeks, scallions—can't be rushed. But that patience is rewarded with tender beans and sweet, sticky caramelized leeks in every bite. Once the beans and leeks are prepared, they can be easily packed into containers and re-frigerated; as you reheat, you may need to loosen up the mixture with a bit of bean broth or water. It'll taste even better the next day.

Leeky Beans on Garlic Toast

MAKES 4 TOASTS

1 tablespoon olive oil, plus more
  for the toast
2 leeks, white and pale green parts only,
  sliced into ¼-inch half-rings
Salt
3 cups Brothy Beans (page 74)

1 clove garlic, sliced in half
4 thick slices good bread
4 handfuls tender baby greens, such as
  arugula, baby kale, or baby spinach
Fresh lemon juice

Warm the olive oil in a medium skillet over medium-low heat, then add the leeks and a few pinches of salt. Cook, stirring periodically, until reduced, sticky, and caramelized, 20 to 30 minutes. Add splashes of water and use a wooden spoon or spatula to scrape up any browned bits as they cook. Stir in the beans and their broth and bring to a simmer.

Toast the bread until crisp. Rub each piece with the garlic and drizzle with a bit of olive oil. Place each piece of toast on a serving plate or in a shallow bowl and spoon the hot beans over the toast.

Toss the greens with a squeeze of lemon juice, a splash of olive oil, and a pinch of salt in a large bowl. Divide the greens over the beans and serve immediately, with a knife and fork.

This simple, summery dip is studded with soft eggplant, smoky charred scallion, and creamy white beans, and I like to make it when I've got access to a grill, which amplifies the smoky element. But since I don't have one, it's more often that I'm using the oven. It's excellent served with crackers and crudités, my favorites being endive leaves, halved radishes, and spears or rounds of cucumber. And while you can blitz everything up in a food processor a la baba ghanoush, I like it better with things chopped and then folded together to allow the independent flavors and textures to shine through. Add a few tablespoons of chopped herbs, like cilantro, dill, or parsley, if you've got them on hand.

Grilled (or Roasted) Eggplant, Scallion, and White Bean Dip

MAKES ABOUT 2 CUPS

1 medium eggplant
1 large or 2 small bunches scallions,
    ends trimmed
2 tablespoons plus a splash of olive oil
¾ cup drained white beans (about half a
    15-ounce can), rinsed if using canned

2 tablespoons well-stirred tahini
Fresh lemon juice
½ teaspoon salt, plus more to taste
Crackers and crudités, for serving

Prick the eggplant all over with a fork or paring knife. Toss the scallions with a splash of olive oil.

Prepare a grill for medium heat, then arrange the eggplant and scallions over indirect heat. The scallions will cook in a minute or two per side; they're done when they take on some char marks and begin to crisp and the white parts are tender. The eggplant will take 10 to 20 minutes, rotated 90 degrees with metal tongs every 3 to 5 minutes, until charred all over, collapsed, and tender all the way through (test by inserting a paring knife into the thickest part of the vegetable).

If you don't have a grill, preheat the oven to 450°F.

Place the eggplant and scallions on opposite ends of a baking sheet and transfer to the oven. Cook the scallions until lightly caramelized and beginning to crisp, 15 to 20 minutes. Transfer them to a cutting board to cool, return the eggplant to the oven, and roast until collapsed and completely tender, another 5 to 15 minutes.

When the eggplant is safe to handle, pull off and discard the skin, then coarsely chop the flesh and transfer to a medium bowl. Coarsely chop the scallions and add to the bowl.

Add the beans to the bowl, along with the 2 tablespoons olive oil, the tahini, a long squeeze of lemon, and the salt. Fold to combine, then taste carefully for seasoning—add salt and additional lemon juice as needed to make all the flavors sing. This dip is best if it has 30 to 60 minutes to sit. Serve at room temperature, with crackers and crudités.

Beans, Canned and Dried

I love the sweet heat in this chili and the luscious texture created by grinding the vegetables and being generous with olive oil. But what I enjoy most might be what happens to the tomatoes: craggy pieces torn by hand are cooked down to velvety slips of their former selves. There's enough flavor here that you really don't need to load it up with traditional chili toppings, but a poached egg on top makes it an even heartier meal. Instructions are included here for cooking the dried beans, but know that it's the same procedure as for the Brothy Beans on page 74—which is to say that if you've got a tub of brothy beans in the fridge, you're only a few steps away from making chili!

Ancho Bean Chili

MAKES 4 QUARTS, ENOUGH TO SERVE 8 TO 10

1 pound medium beans
　　(cannellini, kidney, navy, pinto,
　　cranberry, or a combination),
　　soaked overnight
6 tablespoons olive oil, divided
1 tablespoon plus 1 teaspoon salt
8 plump cloves garlic, coarsely chopped
1 tablespoon tomato paste
1½ tablespoons ground ancho chile
2 teaspoons coriander seeds

1 teaspoon cumin seeds
1 teaspoon fennel seeds
1 large onion, roughly chopped
1 large carrot, roughly chopped
2 bay leaves
2 tablespoons brown sugar
1 cup dry red wine or light,
　　non-hoppy beer
One 28-ounce can whole tomatoes and
　　their juice

Place the beans in a large saucepan and cover with about 2 inches of water. Put over high heat and bring to a boil. Add 3 tablespoons of the olive oil and 1 tablespoon of the salt and reduce the heat to maintain a gentle simmer. Cook, stirring every now and then and skimming off any foam that gathers on the surface. Start checking for doneness after 30 minutes—either by tasting a bean or by cutting it in half. If the beans start to poke above the surface, add more water to keep them just submerged. As you taste, also check for seasoning, adding more salt as needed. Before removing from the heat, make sure to taste several beans, all of which should be thoroughly tender. To store, let cool, then transfer—both the beans and their cooking liquid—to airtight containers and keep in the fridge.

Preheat the oven to 350°F.

Combine the garlic, tomato paste, ancho chile, and coriander, cumin, and fennel seeds in a food processor and process until you have a paste; add a tablespoon of water if necessary to get things moving. Add the onion and carrot and pulse until everything is finely chopped.

Warm the remaining 3 tablespoons oil in a Dutch oven over medium heat, then add the carrot-onion mixture and the bay leaves. Cook, stirring periodically, until the mixture begins to caramelize and stick to the bottom of the pan, 15 to 20 minutes. Stir in the brown sugar and the remaining 1 teaspoon salt, then pour in the wine or beer and scrape up any browned bits from the bottom of the pot. Add the beans and their cooking liquid and the tomatoes, crushing them a bit with a wooden spoon as you add them to the pot. Pour in additional water if needed so that the beans and vegetables are submerged and just able to swim freely. Bring to a boil, then cover and transfer to the oven. Cook for 45 minutes, remove the lid, then cook for 15 minutes more, or until the broth is rich and thick and the craggy pieces of tomato are velvety. Season with salt, if needed, and serve hot.

Having already written a book and had a food business dedicated to veggie burgers, I thought I'd had my share of them. But this recipe revived my appreciation. The entire recipe comes together in a single skillet, and it sings with texture and flavor. I like to serve them traditionally, between buns with traditional burger fixings, but I also like them as something of a vegetable "cake" that functions as the perfect accompaniment to a green salad. I even like them as picnic and car trip food served at room temperature—I sandwich the patties between slices of good bread with some mashed avocado, a slather of mustard, and a few pieces of lettuce.

White Bean and Carrot Burgers

MAKES 4 BURGERS

Olive oil
½ cup panko (1 ounce)
3 shallots, or 1 small onion, diced
1 tablespoon tomato paste
1½ teaspoons salt
1 cup grated carrots (from 2 medium carrots)

1½ tablespoons apple cider vinegar
Two 15-ounce cans cannellini or other white beans, drained and rinsed
1 egg, beaten
Freshly ground black pepper
Burger accompaniments, as suggested above

Heat 1 tablespoon olive oil in a medium skillet over low heat. Add the panko and cook, stirring often, until lightly browned and crisp, 3 to 5 minutes. Transfer to a bowl or plate, then return the pan to the heat.

Add 2 tablespoons olive oil to the skillet, followed by the onion. Cook until softened and lightly golden, 8 to 10 minutes. Stir in the tomato paste, salt, and carrots and stir frequently until the carrots are soft and a bit blistered, another 8 to 10 minutes. Deglaze with the vinegar, scraping up all the browned bits until the pan is dry. Remove from the heat and add the toasted panko and beans. Use a wooden spoon or spatula to very coarsely mash the mixture until a bit pasty and the mixture coheres in places—there should still be plenty of beans intact. Stir in the egg. Shape into 4 patties (a 4-inch ring mold or biscuit cutter makes this quick and easy) or 10 to 12 sliders.

To cook the veggie burgers, heat a thin layer of olive oil in a wide skillet over medium heat and carefully cook until browned and slightly firm to the touch, 3 to 4 minutes per side. It may be necessary to cook in batches. Serve hot or at room temperature, with accompaniments as desired.

A Few Canned Bean Salads

You don't have to use canned beans in these salads, but know that the recipes are designed to be quick-assembly dishes, ones that can be packed up for weekday lunches or put into coolers to go to the park or the beach. Sometimes the thick, starchy liquid in canned beans can be useful in a dish—in particular soups and other cooked dishes where it helps add body—but for these dishes, you'll want to rinse the canned beans before adding them to your salads.

BLACK BEANS WITH SCALLION-LIME VINAIGRETTE, AVOCADO, AND SPINACH

SERVES 3 OR 4

Charred scallions—which appear in several recipes in this book, that's how much I love them—lend a smoky, savory element when they're coarsely chopped and stirred into a vinaigrette. This one is offset with a jolt of lime, and with the greens and avocado, this passes as a main dish salad.

6 scallions, trimmed and sliced lengthwise

2 tablespoons fresh lime juice

½ teaspoon dried oregano

1 teaspoon salt

Pinch sugar

3 tablespoons olive oil

Two 15-ounce cans black beans, drained and rinsed

¾ cup halved cherry tomatoes

1 avocado, cubed

2 big handfuls baby spinach or other tender salad greens

¼ cup crumbled feta cheese (optional)

Place a large skillet over high heat. When hot, add the scallions and press them down with a metal spatula until they char and blister, 5 to 7 minutes. Transfer to a cutting board. When they're safe to handle, coarsely chop them, then combine them with the lime juice, oregano, salt, sugar, and olive oil in a small bowl. Taste and adjust the seasonings if necessary.

Combine the beans, tomatoes, and dressing in a serving bowl—it can sit for a bit and marinate, either at room temperature or in the refrigerator overnight. Just before serving, toss with the avocado, greens, and cheese, if using.

WINTER WHITE BEAN SALAD WITH GRAPEFRUIT

SERVES 4

This salad is exactly what I crave in the winter. It's got texture in the form of crunchy stuff (celery, radishes) and quench in the form of juicy stuff (pieces of grapefruit flesh), and it's so brightly flavored it seems to just glow. Learning how to supreme a citrus—to trim away all the peel and pith as well as the membranes between the fruit segments—isn't hard, but it may be helpful to watch a tutorial on YouTube to see how it's done. For me, citrus prepared this way is one of the most luxurious ways of serving fruit, superior to a peeled grape for sure.

WHITE BEAN, TOMATO,
AND DILL SALAD WITH
CHARRED ROMAINE,
PAGE 93

WINTER WHITE BEAN
SALAD WITH GRAPEFRUIT,
PAGE 89

SMOKY CHICKPEA SALAD
WITH OLIVES AND LEMON,
PAGE 92

BLACK BEANS WITH
SCALLION-LIME VINAIGRETTE,
AVOCADO, AND SPINACH,
PAGE 89

¼ red onion, thinly sliced

¾ teaspoon salt, plus more as needed

1 tablespoon red or white wine vinegar

1 grapefruit

Two 15-ounce cans cannellini or other white beans, drained and rinsed

3 stalks celery, thinly sliced

6 big radishes, cut into quarters or cubes

2 tablespoons olive oil

Freshly ground black pepper

Handful of mint, parsley, or cilantro leaves (optional)

In a serving bowl, toss the onion with the salt, then add the vinegar. Let stand for a few minutes as you prepare the rest of the salad.

On a cutting board, trim all the peel and pith from the grapefruit. Holding the fruit over the serving bowl, cut the fruit segments away from the membranes, collecting both the juices and the grapefruit flesh in the bowl. Squeeze any remaining juice from the spent grapefruit membrane into the bowl, then discard it. Pick out any seeds and break the fruit into smaller, bite-size pieces.

Stir in the beans, celery, radishes, olive oil, and a few grinds of black pepper. Taste and season with salt. Just before serving, add the herbs, if using.

SMOKY CHICKPEA SALAD WITH OLIVES AND LEMON

SERVES 4 AS A SIDE

For this salad, you'll first create a super-flavorful oil, in which you've bloomed smoked paprika and added aromatic lemon zest and garlic to sizzle. Then it gets poured over the beans, cloaking them in flavor. Just before serving, whole parsley leaves are folded in—they mimic salad greens but have much more flavor. Add a split soft-boiled egg on the side and you've got a very satisfying lunch.

1 lemon

3 tablespoons olive oil

3 cloves garlic, sliced

12 good olives, such as Kalamata or Castelvetrano, pitted and coarsely chopped or torn

¾ teaspoon smoked paprika

Pinch red pepper flakes

Two 15-ounce cans chickpeas, rinsed and drained

¾ teaspoon salt

Freshly ground black pepper

½ cup whole parsley leaves

Use a vegetable peeler to remove 3 thick strips of zest from the lemon. Combine them with the olive oil, garlic, olives, smoked paprika, and red pepper flakes in a small skillet and set over low heat. Let warm and gently sizzle for 5 to 10 minutes, until the garlic is tender.

Place the chickpeas in a large bowl. Pour the oil and contents of the skillet over the chickpeas and add the salt and several grinds of black pepper. Add half of the juice from the lemon, taste, and add more if necessary. Before serving, toss with the parsley leaves. You won't eat the lemon peel, but I usually leave it in the serving dish for decoration if dishing out at the table. Serve warm or at room temperature.

WHITE BEAN, TOMATO, AND DILL SALAD WITH CHARRED ROMAINE

SERVES 4

I love lettuce, mostly because I find it so quenching and its crunch—in the case of greens like romaine—to be so satisfying. But when you apply heat to lettuce, new flavors appear and it becomes succulent. This is a centerpiece salad, where each diner gets a charred romaine half with a fresh, verdant-tasting bean salad spooned over. Note that this salad is pretty heavy on the dill, so if you're not a huge fan, you may want to dial it down a notch.

1 shallot, minced

2 tablespoons red or white wine vinegar

1 teaspoon salt

Two 15-ounce cans cannellini beans, drained and rinsed

1 cup coarsely chopped dill

1 cup halved cherry tomatoes, or 1 ripe tomato, chopped

3 tablespoons olive oil

Freshly ground black pepper

2 tight romaine hearts, split lengthwise

Thin slabs of feta cheese (optional)

Combine the shallot, vinegar, and salt in a large bowl and let stand for about 10 minutes. Add the beans, dill, tomatoes, oil, and plenty of black pepper. Adjust the seasonings to taste—the flavors develop a bit as the salad sits.

Set a gas stovetop burner flame on high. Using tongs, and working one at a time, set the romaine halves directly over the flame, cut-side down, and allow the lettuce heads to blister and char all over their cut sides. Move them over the flame as necessary for even charring. This will take less than 90 seconds. (Alternatively, char the lettuce over the high heat of a grill or under the broiler set to high heat.)

To serve, place the lettuce, cut-side up, on plates or a platter and spoon the bean salad on top of it. Serve with the cheese alongside, if using. You could also coarsely chop the romaine and fold it into the beans for easier packing (as pictured on page 90). Serve warm or at room temperature.

CHAPTER 8

A Few Sweet Potatoes

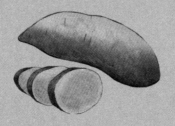

Growing up, I only ever remember eating sweet potatoes in puree form, from jars of Gerber baby food. Although during the holidays, my grandmother would use the whole vegetable to make candied "yams" (they were sweet potatoes, not yams) using her West Bend electric skillet. We just didn't eat them otherwise. It turns out that period (the eighties and nineties) was a low point for sweet potato production, when the peaking industrialization of produce nudged them out of popularity. But thanks to the low-carb diets of the early aughts, which promoted the vegetable's nutritional profile (they're low-carb, rich in beta-carotene, and brimming with vitamins and minerals), demand for sweet potatoes increased, causing production to increase as well—and the popularity of the sweet potato as a health food has surged. There doesn't seem to be any sign of sweet potatoes retreating back into the shadows.

You'll often find a few different varieties at the supermarket. White-fleshed sweet potatoes (Japanese sweet potatoes are one such type) are a bit starchier and less sweet than their orange-fleshed counterparts. There are also purple-fleshed ones, which have gained some fame in the Instagram era. In all cases, sweet potatoes are an assertive vegetable. Even if you wanted to, you probably couldn't conceal their nutty, caramel-sweet flavor, so it's best to put them in dishes where they'll be allowed to shine. They stand up to, and pair well with, bold flavors, as the following recipes attest: think tahini, miso paste, thick plain yogurt, toasted sesame oil.

It's very likely sweet potatoes are already a fixture in your cooking, and you have a favorite way to cook them. But as I suggest in the first recipe of this chapter, I think it's worth reconsidering your go-to method and giving them the low-and-slow oven treatment. I first learned about this from Michael Solomonov's *Zahav* cookbook. He cooks sweet potatoes for two and a half hours on very low heat, until the flesh is custardy and deeply caramelized inside, and then blisters the salty skins under a broiler. They're a real treat that way. Lowering the temperature and increasing the cooking time made a noticeable difference from the high-heat method I used to use: more richly flavored flesh and a less stringy, soft, spoonable texture that needs very little embellishment.

But there are merits to higher heat cooking, too, which include: sweet potato fries and roasting broad slabs that then go into an SPLT (a sweet potato, lettuce, and tomato sandwich). And they integrate beautifully in soups and stews and cook quickly along with any other complementary ingredients in the pot.

Unlike russets and other types of potatoes, sweet potatoes aren't really a cold storage crop and are more delicate than they seem. The skins are thin and the flesh bruises easily. So don't stock up on more than a week or so worth of sweet potatoes when you go shopping, keep them in a cool and dry place in your kitchen, and try not to bang them around too much.

Give this sweet potato cooking method a try—the lower temperature and longer cooking time yields softer, more flavorful flesh—and then make extras so that you have them at the ready later in the week. In all the recipes that follow, where "gently roasted sweet potatoes" are called for, you can roast them however you please, or even cook them in a pressure cooker like the Instant Pot.

Gently Roasted Sweet Potatoes

MAKES AS MANY SWEET POTATOES AS YOU'D LIKE TO COOK

Sweet potatoes
Olive oil
Salt

Preheat the oven to 300°F.

Arrange the sweet potatoes in a baking dish or on a baking sheet. Drizzle with a small amount of olive oil and rub over all the skins. Sprinkle with salt. Transfer to the oven and bake for 60 to 90 minutes, or more, until completely tender—the sweet potatoes will have shrunk inside their skins a bit and a paring knife inserted into the flesh will meet no resistance. They're ready to eat while hot, or after they have cooled, they can be stored in an airtight container in the refrigerator for 3 to 5 days.

To reheat, place the sweet potato(es) in a preheated 325°F oven for 15 to 20 minutes. Or to reheat them in the microwave, microwave on high for 1 minute, and then in 30-second increments until warmed through.

Here's a stuffed baked potato reimagined. Instead of cheese and sour cream there's savory miso butter and then a pile of tender greens. The greens wilt just slightly as you mix them into the warm sweet potatoes. I find this to be a perfect light vegetarian main when I'm coming home from a long day (reheat a cooked sweet potato in the oven or toaster oven at 350°F for about 15 minutes), and it goes nicely with a cup of hot, brothy soup. If you've got Marinated Greens (page 54) on hand, swap them for the tender greens.

Sweet Potato with Miso Butter and Greens

SERVES 1, EASILY MULTIPLIED

1 tablespoon butter, softened
1 teaspoon light-colored miso paste
1 Gently Roasted Sweet Potato (page 97),
   hot

1 handful tender greens, such as arugula,
   baby spinach, or baby kale
Flaky salt
Freshly ground black pepper
Lemon zest (optional)

In a small bowl, mash together the butter and miso paste.

Split open the sweet potato and give it a gentle squeeze to expose some of the flesh. Top with the miso butter, then tuck the greens into the sweet potato jacket, mixing them with the sweet potato a bit. Garnish with salt, black pepper, and a swipe or two of lemon zest, if using.

Here's a fun, cheffy-looking salad with a wonderful layering of flavors and textures: cool, creamy yogurt; cold chunks of sweet potato; and a warm, intensely flavored oil that's spooned over everything just before serving. Try sheep's milk yogurt, which has a much more pronounced tang. Or stir a little water into thick strained yogurt, such as Greek yogurt, to lighten it up and give it a fluffier consistency. The seed topping is also delicious spooned over rice or roasted vegetables, or as a dipping sauce for bread.

Cold Sweet Potatoes with Spiced Seeds and Yogurt

SERVES 4

1 tablespoon olive oil
¼ white onion, finely minced
1 teaspoon coriander seeds, crushed
1 teaspoon salt
Pinch red pepper flakes

¼ cup raw sunflower seeds
½ cup plain yogurt
2 Gently Roasted Sweet Potatoes
    (page 97), chilled, peeled, and cubed
2 teaspoons toasted sesame oil

Warm the oil in a small skillet over medium-low heat and add the onion, coriander seeds, salt, and red pepper flakes. Cook until the onion is soft and beginning to caramelize, 6 to 8 minutes—it may even crisp a bit, which isn't a bad thing; just don't let it burn. Stir in the sunflower seeds and continue cooking, stirring often, until they're fragrant and lightly browned, another 6 to 8 minutes or so.

Spread the yogurt over a serving plate, then pile the cubed sweet potatoes on top. Sprinkle with the seed mixture and drizzle with the toasted sesame oil. Serve immediately, to show off the contrasts of the cold yogurt, cold sweet potatoes, and warm seed topping.

This loaf has a good dose of sesame seeds, which not only imbue it with nutty perfume but give it a striking visual look. Play it up by using a combination of black and white sesame seeds. You can substitute canned pumpkin or butternut squash for the sweet potato, if you'd like—you'll need 1 cup—and while the flavor of a mild olive oil isn't pronounced, if you don't enjoy the taste of olive oil in your baked goods, a vegetable or canola oil can be substituted. And a "flax egg" makes this a vegan loaf: whisk 2 tablespoons ground flax seed with 6 tablespoons water and let the mixture sit for 20 to 30 minutes to thicken, then add to the batter where you would the eggs, as directed below.

Sesame Sweet Potato Loaf

MAKES ONE 8½ X 4½-INCH LOAF

1 Gently Roasted Sweet Potato
  (page 97; about 12 ounces before
  roasting), or 1 cup sweet potato puree
⅔ cup sugar
½ cup olive oil
2 eggs
3 tablespoons water
½ teaspoon vanilla extract

1½ cups all-purpose flour
¼ cup plus 1 tablespoon toasted
  sesame seeds, divided
1 teaspoon baking soda
½ teaspoon salt
1 tablespoon turbinado (raw) sugar,
  or granulated sugar

Preheat the oven to 325°F. Grease an 8½ x 4½-inch loaf pan and line it with a strip of parchment paper that hangs over the sides.

Remove the peel from the roasted sweet potato, then place it in a food processor and process until smooth. Add the sugar, olive oil, eggs, water, and vanilla and pulse to combine. Scrape the sides with a spatula and pulse once more. Whisk together the flour, ¼ cup of the sesame seeds, the baking soda, and salt in a large bowl, then fold the sweet potato mixture into the dry ingredients. Scrape into the prepared pan and sprinkle with the turbinado sugar followed by the remaining 1 tablespoon sesame seeds.

Transfer to the oven and bake for 60 to 70 minutes, until set in the center and a tester comes out clean, rotating the pan once halfway through. Cool in the pan for 15 minutes, then lift out with the parchment ends and let cool completely on a rack before slicing.

If you google "sweet potato toast," the leading results are recipes in which the sweet potato, cut into a slab and seared, *is* the toast. That's not the case here. When sweet potatoes are cooked to custardy, caramelized perfection, the flesh can be spread thickly on a good piece of bread. Think of it as sweet potato butter. Here are options to take it in either sweet or savory directions.

Sweet Potato Toast, Sweet or Savory

MAKES 1 TOAST

Sweet
2 teaspoons sugar
¼ teaspoon ground cinnamon
1 thick slice good bread
Butter or coconut oil

About ½ medium Gently Roasted
Sweet Potato (page 97), peeled
Flaky salt

Mix together the sugar and cinnamon in a small bowl.

Toast the bread until crisp and golden brown. While warm, spread with butter or coconut oil, then smear the sweet potato over it. Sprinkle with the cinnamon-sugar mix (you may not want to use all of it).

Preheat the broiler (if your toaster oven has a broiler function, use that), then place under the broiler and cook until lightly browned. Sprinkle with salt and serve hot, with a knife and fork.

Savory
1 thick slice good bread
About ½ medium Gently Roasted
Sweet Potato (page 97), peeled
Olive oil
1 egg

Salt
Freshly ground black pepper
Sriracha
Tahini

Toast the bread until crisp and golden brown. Smear the sweet potato flesh over it.

Meanwhile, warm a thin film of olive oil in a small skillet over medium heat. Crack in the egg. Sprinkle with salt and black pepper and cook until the white is set and the yolk is cooked to your liking. Use a spatula to place the egg on top of the sweet potato. Drizzle with sriracha and tahini to taste. Serve hot, with a knife and fork.

These sweet potato chips look so unassuming. They're baked, of course, which elicits skepticism, and they get a little splotched with dark spots as they crisp in the oven. And then there are always a few that don't quite get crisp, that are what my brother and I used to call "Sloppy Joes"—the limp, oily, super salty fries at the bottom of the McDonald's bag (those ones were our favorites). But every time I make them, they disappear immediately. Any of the seasoned salts on page 234 would work well here in place of the lime salt.

Baked Sweet Potato Chips

MAKES ENOUGH FOR 4 AS A SIDE

2 medium sweet potatoes
(about 12 ounces each)
2 tablespoons olive oil

1 teaspoon flaky salt
Pinch crushed red pepper flakes
Zest of 1 lime

Preheat the oven to 425°F.

Using a mandoline or, if you don't have one, a chef's knife, slice the sweet potatoes into rounds about ⅛ inch thick. Place in a large bowl, add the oil, and stir to coat evenly. Arrange on a baking sheet in the best single layer you can manage, then transfer to the oven and bake for 10 minutes. Stir and flip, then return to the oven and bake for 5 to 10 minutes more, until most of the chips are crisp and browned (some may take on some black spots; that's fine). Watch carefully toward the end, as they darken quickly.

In a small bowl, mix together the salt and red pepper flakes. Sprinkle over the sweet potato chips and zest the lime over everything. Serve while they're still warm. These are best eaten within a few hours.

My favorite part of this salad is the dressing, where deeply flavored roasted shallots (or onion) are chopped up and form the basis of an astonishingly good vinaigrette made from otherwise ordinary pantry ingredients. It really screams "Autumn!" with the roasted sweet potatoes, apple, and toasted pecans, and is the kind of salad I'm always hoping to find at the Thanksgiving table.

Roasted Sweet Potato Salad

SERVES 4 TO 6 AS A SIDE

2 medium sweet potatoes
3 shallots, peeled and halved through
    the stem, or ½ medium onion,
    cut into 4 wedges
3 tablespoons olive oil, plus more for
    roasting the sweet potatoes
Salt
2 tablespoons apple cider vinegar
½ teaspoon honey

Salt
Freshly ground black pepper
½ cup toasted walnuts or pecans,
    coarsely chopped
½ cup cubed sharp cheddar cheese
1 tart apple, cored and cubed
4 cups baby arugula or other spicy,
    tender green (4 handfuls)

Preheat the oven to 425°F.

Arrange the sweet potatoes and shallots or onion on a baking sheet. Drizzle with olive oil and sprinkle with salt and use your hands to coat. Transfer to the oven and roast until the shallots are softened and caramelized, 10 to 15 minutes, then remove them from the pan. Return the sweet potatoes to the oven and bake until tender and a bit blistered, another 10 to 15 minutes.

To make the dressing, finely chop the roasted shallot or onion (once it's safe to handle) and place in a small bowl or jar. Cover with the vinegar, honey, and a big pinch of salt, then stir in the 3 tablespoons olive oil. Season with black pepper and additional salt as needed.

To assemble the salad, combine the warm or cooled potatoes with the nuts, cheese, apple, and arugula, then toss with most of the dressing, adding more to taste if needed (you may have some dressing left over).

This soup has a decadent richness that skeptics of vegan cooking are often surprised by (tahini can pull a lot of weight!). It also comes together in about thirty minutes, making it a great option for weeknights. You'll notice that I call for water rather than stock; in this recipe, it makes for a better liquid, as it keeps the flavors of the soup pure and aligned. Frizzled shallots make an excellent, if optional, garnish.

Sweet Potato and Tahini Soup

SERVES 4 TO 6

2 tablespoons olive oil
1 onion, chopped
4 cloves garlic, sliced
1 tablespoon minced or grated ginger
1½ teaspoons ground coriander
¾ teaspoon ground cumin
1½ teaspoons salt, divided

3 medium sweet potatoes, peeled and
    sliced into thin rounds or half-rounds
    (1½ to 2 pounds)
2 tablespoons well-stirred tahini
Fresh lemon juice
Frizzled Shallots (recipe follows; optional)

Warm the olive oil over medium heat in a soup pot or Dutch oven, then add the onion, garlic, ginger, coriander, cumin, and ½ teaspoon of the salt. Cook until the onion is soft and beginning to caramelize, 6 to 8 minutes. Add the sweet potatoes, raise the heat slightly, and stir until they're glistening all over, another 3 to 4 minutes. Cover with 5 cups water. Bring to a simmer and add the remaining 1 teaspoon salt. Cook for about 15 minutes, until the sweet potatoes are tender. Add the soup to a blender with the tahini, in batches if necessary, and puree. (You can also use an immersion blender, but be thorough to achieve a properly smooth consistency.) Return to the pot to rewarm, add lemon juice and additional salt to taste, and serve hot, with frizzled shallots, if you like.

Frizzled Shallots

Vegetable, grapeseed, or canola oil,
    for frying

5 small or 3 large shallots, sliced into
    paper-thin wisps on a mandoline
Salt

Heat about ¼ inch of oil in a small skillet over medium heat. Dip a ring of shallot into it to ensure it's properly hot—it will sizzle immediately when it's ready—then add the rest of them. Cook until they get crisp and turn a reddish-brown color, 10 to 20 minutes. Watch carefully once they start to color, as they can burn easily. Use a slotted spoon to transfer them to a paper towel–lined plate to drain. Sprinkle with salt. Save the oil—strain it through a coffee filter and then use it in salad dressings where you want a savory kick!

An easy, hearty, and broadly pleasing stew-slash-soup made from cheap ingredients is always welcome in my cooking repertoire. Here, from the color, to the texture, to the blank canvas for flavors, sweet potatoes complement red lentils in every way, and caramelized onions deglazed with a good splash of vinegar give the soup some tangy distinction. If you wish to skip the salad as a topping, you can just as easily stir the greens into the soup at the end, allowing them to wilt; in that case, serve with lemon wedges on the side and a drizzle of olive oil on top.

Red Lentil and Sweet Potato Stew

SERVES 4

3 tablespoons olive oil, plus more for
    drizzling
1 large white or yellow onion, diced
1½ teaspoons salt, divided
3 tablespoons apple cider vinegar
4 cloves garlic, minced
1 tablespoon finely grated ginger
2 medium sweet potatoes
    (about 12 ounces each), peeled and
    diced

1⅓ cups red lentils, rinsed and drained
5 ounces tender greens, such as
    spinach or baby kale, or shredded kale
    or Swiss chard
Juice from ½ lemon, to taste
Plain yogurt or nondairy yogurt,
    for serving

In a soup pot or Dutch oven, warm the oil over medium heat. Add the onions and ½ teaspoon of the salt and cook until golden and caramelized, 20 to 30 minutes. Add the vinegar, stir to scrape up any browned bits from the pot, and allow to reduce by half.

Stir the garlic and ginger into the pot, then add the sweet potatoes and lentils. Stir to coat in the oil, then cover with 6 cups water. Bring to a boil, reduce the heat to a simmer, and add the remaining 1 teaspoon salt. Cook, partially covered, until the sweet potatoes and lentils are tender, about 20 minutes. Taste for seasoning.

Just before serving, toss the greens in a medium bowl with a few spritzes of lemon juice, a pinch of salt, and a drizzle of olive oil.

Ladle the hot soup into bowls and divide the dressed greens on top. Serve with dollops of yogurt.

No one will confuse a sweet potato for bacon in a BLT, but in this classic sandwich it holds its own. I use cherry tomatoes here, because supermarkets carry them all year long and they taste significantly better than mealy off-season standard tomatoes. If tomatoes are in season, use a ripe, juicy one—your sandwich will be that much better. If you don't eat eggs, vegan mayonnaise is excellent in place of the traditional variety.

SPLT (Sweet Potato, Lettuce, and Tomato)

MAKES 2 SANDWICHES

1 medium sweet potato
1 tablespoon olive oil
2 teaspoons maple syrup
Salt
Freshly ground black pepper
4 slices of your favorite sandwich bread

Mayonnaise (egg-based or vegan)
½ cup halved or quartered cherry
    tomatoes
Red wine vinegar
Crisp lettuce (romaine, iceberg,
    butter leaf)

Preheat the oven to 425°F.

Trim the ends off the sweet potato, then slice it into lengthwise slabs about ½ inch thick. Arrange them on a baking sheet and use your hands to coat them with the olive oil and maple syrup, plus a liberal sprinkling of salt and black pepper. Transfer to the oven and cook until tender and splotched, flipping them once halfway through, about 25 minutes.

Toast the bread and spread each piece with mayo. Divide the cherry tomatoes on top of two slices. Sprinkle with salt and black pepper and a splash of vinegar. Shingle the sweet potatoes over the tomatoes, then top with lettuce. Close the sandwiches, slice in half, and eat right away, while the bread is still warm.

CHAPTER 9

A Carton of Eggs

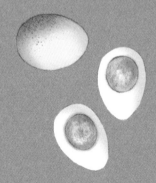

I love watching people cook eggs, because everyone has their own method. My brother, Max, greases an electric griddle and carefully fries eggs on one end of it, while the other toasts buttered English muffins facedown—he makes the best breakfast sandwiches. Once I watched the chef Elise Kornack heat up a carbon-steel pan in her home kitchen for what seemed like twenty minutes, then cracked a single egg straight into the very hot oiled pan and scrambled it with a spoon in a matter of seconds—this was breakfast for her wife, Anna. My stepmom, Pam, seems to engage her whole body as she fries an egg, swirling the pan and turning a spatula so as to encase a perfectly runny yolk in a perfectly set white, mastering the challenge of getting both cooked at the same pace (if you go to YouTube and search for "perfect fried egg," there are French chefs who've spent their careers mastering a method not dissimilar to this).

I eat eggs often, and the first reason I like them is that they're delicious. They do offer a boost of protein and iron, plus numerous vitamins and minerals, but there's constant debate over how healthy they are, plagued as they were by decades of fear of cholesterol. The current research indicates that much of the basis for the cholesterol scare has been debunked, which is not to say that one should eat eggs with abandon, but rather that, like most foods, they're best regarded as a component of a balanced meal, ideally one that features a hearty dose of vegetables. Eggs are a default of mine when I need something to eat *now*, getting home late and hungry, or wanting a hearty breakfast, or even a snack. I was an early adopter of #putaneggonit, the Instagram movement of taking any manner of savory dish and topping it with a fried, poached, or soft-boiled egg, its vibrant yellow yolk dripping in dramatically photogenic fashion.

What I aim to do in this chapter is offer you some new ideas for eggs, since I'm guessing you have default recipes and methods of your own. From a collection of unusual ways to cook them, simple techniques meant to help you out of egg-cooking ruts, to five vegetable-laden egg-on-toasts (because there are few things better than egg on toast), these recipes capitalize on what I find to be so appealing about having eggs around—which is that you're just a few steps from a meal. From there a few types of baked eggs offer dishes that are both brunch- and dinner-worthy, satisfying meals that need just a salad and some steamed rice or bread to round them out.

With eggs, it's worth buying the best ones you can afford, from producers invested in the livelihood of their chickens. Otherwise the world of industrialized egg production is a grim system to be participating in. And as an added benefit, these humanely raised eggs typically have more vibrantly colored yolks (the color of the yolk is determined by their diets—grass makes a yolk more yellow) and taste better, too. The colors of the shells tell you very little about the chickens except that white-feathered hens lay white eggs, and red- and brown-feathered chickens lay brown eggs. The more important information can be relayed by the farmer, who'll be able to vouch for farm conditions, or on the packaging, look for "cage-free," "free-range," or "pasture-raised."

This is one of those quick meals that feels like self-care, squarely in the category of invalid food. A flavorful poached egg sits atop a crisp slab of toasted bread that's resting in a little pool of hot broth. You can make your own court bouillon (a quick form of stock) from pantry-staple vegetables and lingering vegetable scraps (see the recipe below), but I'm also a fan of good-quality, store-bought vegetable bouillon such as Better Than Bouillon. I use it in a smaller ratio of bouillon to water than the package recommends—I prefer a heaping ½ teaspoon to 1 cup water. This isn't soup, and you won't use all of the broth when serving. But you can easily multiply the recipe, cooking eggs in the broth and straining it of any debris before ladling it into the bowls.

Broth-Poached Egg over Toast

SERVES 1, EASILY MULTIPLIED

2 cups seasoned broth
Salt
1 egg
1 thick slice good bread

Olive oil
About 1 tablespoon chopped herbs: parsley,
    dill, chives (optional)
Freshly ground black pepper

Bring the broth to a simmer in a small pot and taste it for seasoning—you'll be eating it, so make sure it tastes good! Crack the egg into a small bowl (such as a ramekin or a Pyrex), then gently lower into the simmering liquid and immediately use a spoon to stir around the egg so that the white curls around the yolk. Cook for 2 to 4 minutes, until the yolk is cooked how you like, then remove from the broth using a slotted spoon.

Meanwhile, toast the bread well. Place it in a shallow bowl and drizzle with a bit of olive oil.

Place the egg on top of the toast, then ladle about ½ cup of the broth over. Sprinkle with the herbs and a few grinds of black pepper, then serve.

Quick Court Bouillon

1 teaspoon olive oil
1 small or ½ medium white or yellow
    onion, chopped
1 small carrot, chopped
2 cloves garlic, smashed
1 bay leaf
2 whole peppercorns

Optional vegetable scraps: 3 asparagus
    ends, small handful mushroom stems,
    1 chopped leek green (in place of the
    onion), shells from shelling peas, small
    handful parsley stems
Big pinch of salt, plus more as needed

In a medium saucepan, warm the olive oil over medium heat, then add the remaining ingredients and salt. Cook the vegetables for 6 to 8 minutes, until they just begin to soften, then pour in 5 cups water. Bring to a boil, then lower the heat and simmer for about 20 minutes, until reduced by about a third. Strain out the solids, then taste and season with another pinch of salt if necessary. This is best used on the day it's made.

This is the way I like to fry my eggs if I'm using them to top leftover fried rice or a grain bowl that has some Asian flavors (miso, soy sauce, ginger, etc.). It's also excellent served simply over hot steamed rice and with a splattering of hot sauce—peak comfort food as far as I'm concerned. Make sure to use the peppery, buttery soy sauce liquid left in the pan, drizzling it over the fried egg and whatever else you might be enjoying with it.

Soy Sauce–Basted Eggs

MAKES 2 EGGS

1 to 2 tablespoons butter

2 eggs

Freshly ground black pepper

2 teaspoons soy sauce

Place a small skillet over medium heat, then add the butter. Once it melts and foaming subsides, carefully crack the eggs into the pan and grind a bit of black pepper over them. Cook until the whites are mostly beginning to set, 30 to 45 seconds, then sprinkle with the soy sauce and cover the pan (with a lid, if you have one, or you can set a larger skillet or baking sheet on top). Cook for about a minute more, until the yolks are set to the doneness you like, then transfer to plates, drizzle with any liquid remaining in the pan, and serve.

This is a fun method of making eggs, taking a plain omelet and turning it into something that draws attention. You separate the eggs and beat the whites to stiff peaks, then fold them into the yolks—and the result is something like a soufflé, something like an omelet. It's also known as an omelet Mousseline, in which case it's often taken in a sweet direction, with a sprinkling of sugar and fruit preserves on the side. I've opted to keep it savory here, and you can take liberties with the fillings as long as they don't weigh down the eggs. Finely grated hard cheese and/or chopped herbs are ideal.

Souffléd Omelet

MAKES 1 OMELET

3 eggs
1 tablespoon butter
¼ teaspoon salt
Optional additions: 2 tablespoons finely grated Parmesan or other assertive

hard cheese; 3 tablespoons minced chives, parsley, basil, or other herbs; hot sauce for finishing
Freshly ground black pepper

Preheat the oven to 375°F.

Separate the eggs. The most efficient and failsafe way to do this is by working over a bowl: Crack the eggs into your hand and shake off the white, then drop the yolk into a second bowl. Make sure that no yolk seeps into the whites and that the bowl used for the whites is clean; otherwise they won't whip to peaks.

Place a small oven-safe skillet over medium heat.

Beat the whites to soft peaks, either by hand or using an electric mixer. Quickly whisk the yolks together, season with salt, then fold the whites in, followed by any optional additions.

Add the butter to the skillet (you can add less butter if using a nonstick skillet), then scrape the egg mixture into the pan, smoothing the top. Cook until just set around the outside, 60 to 90 seconds, then transfer to the oven. Bake until puffed, lightly golden, and just set in the center, 9 to 12 minutes. Gently slide the omelet onto a plate, dust with black pepper, and race it to the table to serve while still hot and before it deflates.

Years ago, an Instagram friend of mine, Elaine S., casually mentioned this genius way of using up leftover polenta. I'd posted a photo of an egg scramble, one where I'd cubed leftover polenta and combined it with a bunch of other leftovers along with a few scrambled eggs. Her tip was to crumble leftover polenta into beaten eggs as they cook in the pan, adding something like faux curds. I love the way the textures mingle—the soft eggs with little pillows of polenta breaking things up, and how it stretches the eggs to a more substantial meal. Adding cheese is a way to enrich the dish.

Scrambled Eggs with Crumbled Polenta

SERVES 2

4 eggs
1 tablespoon olive oil or butter
About ½ cup crumbled leftover polenta
2 tablespoons crumbled goat cheese
    (optional)

2 tablespoons minced parsley or chives
    (optional)
Salt
Freshly ground black pepper

Crack the eggs into a bowl and use a fork to mix until combined.

Place a small skillet over medium-low heat. Warm the oil or melt the butter, then scrape in the eggs. Stir periodically, until about half the egg mixture has become curds, then crumble in the polenta and continue stirring until the eggs are cooked to your liking. Remove from the heat and fold in the cheese and herbs, if using. Sprinkle with salt and black pepper and serve hot.

In this perfect brunch dish, eggs are baked in a bed of kimchi and wilted greens that emanate tangy-spicy-savory flavor. Serve with toast or steamed rice—some starch on the side helps to balance the bite of the kimchi a bit. You'll use "kimchi brine" as a vinegar-like ingredient here—it's simply the liquid that collects in the jar as the vegetables ferment. Tip the jar over a small bowl while holding the kimchi in place, gently pressing on it to extract the liquid.

Eggs Baked in Kimchi

SERVES 2

1 tablespoon butter or olive oil, plus more
    for greasing
¼ medium onion, sliced into strips
Salt
½ cup drained kimchi, coarsely chopped

1 packed cup stemmed Swiss chard,
    chopped into bite-size pieces, or
    mature spinach leaves
2 eggs
1 teaspoon kimchi brine (see headnote)
1 teaspoon toasted sesame oil
Freshly ground black pepper

Preheat the oven to 350°F. Grease two ramekins or one small oven-safe skillet with butter or brush with olive oil.

In a medium skillet, melt the butter or warm the olive oil over medium heat. Add the onion and a pinch of salt and cook until the onion is just softened, about 5 minutes. Add the kimchi and cook until it begins to brown a bit and the pan dries, then add the greens and cook until they're soft and wilted. Transfer the mixture to the small skillet or divide between the prepared ramekins.

If using ramekins, carefully crack an egg into each one. If using a skillet, make two little divots in the kimchi mixture and carefully crack an egg into each one. Drizzle with the kimchi brine and sesame oil and dust with black pepper. Transfer to the oven and bake until the whites are just set but the yolk is still runny, 10 to 15 minutes.

I once worked at a restaurant where we hard-cooked our eggs using a little machine that you'd fill with a bit of water, arrange a half dozen eggs in the basket that fit into the top portion of the contraption, then cover it and set a timer. I'd never seen one and was transfixed—it was sort of like a rice cooker, cooking eggs by controlled-temperature steam. Sure, there isn't anything too tricky about cooking eggs in a pot of water, but steaming uses less water and allows the water to come to simmer faster (and some people on the internet believe it makes the eggs easier to peel—unfortunately, I haven't found this to be true).

Steamed Eggs

VARIED YIELD

Eggs, cold

Fill a saucepan with ½ inch of water, then fit it with a steaming insert (if you don't have a steaming insert, you can skip it; the insert is just a bit of insurance for preventing the eggs from rattling around too much and cracking). Place over high heat and bring the water to a boil. Lower the heat to maintain an active simmer, then use tongs to gently add as many eggs as you'd like and/or will fit in a single layer. Cover and steam for 9 minutes for a jammy yolk, 12 minutes for a firmer one. Halt the cooking by transferring the eggs to an ice bath.

Dressed-up Boiled or Steamed Eggs

OLIVE OIL, S&P: While the egg(s) is still warm, peel and halve it, then drizzle with good olive oil and sprinkle with flaky salt and freshly ground black pepper. So simple, but it ain't broke.

SEED-SLICKED: Mix together equal parts sesame and flax seeds (or use a pre-made everything spice blend), and spread out in a thin layer on a small plate. Slice the egg(s) in half lengthwise and rub each surface with a bit of olive oil. Dip in the seeds so that the seeds coat the surface.

SOY SAUCE AND GINGER: Slice the egg(s) in half lengthwise and place, cut-side up, on a plate. Finely grate a bit of peeled ginger over each piece, then drizzle with soy sauce. Add a little thinly sliced scallion, if you like.

TAHINI-YOGURT SAUCE: Stir together three parts plain yogurt (3 teaspoons, for example) to one part tahini (1 teaspoon), then whisk in small amounts of water, if needed, to lighten the consistency. Put a smear of the sauce on a small plate. Slice the egg(s) in half lengthwise and arrange on top. Drizzle with a bit of olive oil and sprinkle with salt and black pepper.

This is a favorite breakfast-for-dinner omelet, and it perfectly illustrates cooking as a matter of component building. Here you've got pickled onions, an easy tahini-yogurt sauce, and tender greens, all tucked inside an omelet that takes less three minutes to throw together once those components are laid out before you. If you don't have marinated greens on hand, just wilt a few handfuls of baby spinach or other tender greens, press them to extract excess liquid, and season them with a few pinches of salt.

Omelet with Greens, Pickled Onions, and Tahini-Yogurt Sauce

MAKES 1 OMELET

¼ small red onion, sliced into strips
(scant ¼ cup)
Salt
1 tablespoon red wine vinegar
1½ teaspoons well-stirred tahini
1 tablespoon plain yogurt

2 eggs
Splash of olive oil
½ cup Marinated Greens
(page 54, or see headnote)
Freshly ground black pepper

Mix together the onions and ¼ teaspoon salt in a small bowl until glistening, then add the vinegar and let stand for about 5 minutes.

In a separate bowl, stir together the tahini and yogurt. If needed, add water by the teaspoon to thin it to a creamy consistency. Season with a pinch of salt. In a third bowl, whisk together the eggs.

Heat a small skillet—ideally a nonstick omelet pan—over medium heat. Add a splash of oil (if not using nonstick, a thin film to coat the bottom of the pan) and then scrape in the eggs. Cook, working around the perimeter of the eggs by tipping the pan and gently lifting the omelet with a rubber spatula to allow uncooked egg to run underneath, until the eggs are mostly set. Arrange the greens over one half, followed by the drained onions and the tahini sauce. Sprinkle with salt and black pepper. Slide onto a plate, folding the unfilled part of the omelet over the fillings, and serve immediately.

Crispy, coarse breadcrumbs, tender slow-cooked kale, runny-yolked eggs, and a bracing dash of vinegar: This is an excellent brunch dish that's endlessly adaptable for your greens—adjust the cooking time as necessary (I call for kale and spinach here, and find that it's best when cooked low and slow). You'll taste the vinegar in this dish, so try to use a good-quality one. And to speed things up, you can certainly use pre-made Marinated Greens (page 54). Simply rewarm them before adding the eggs and sliding the pan into the oven; you'll need about 1 heaping cup.

Eggs in Greens with Breadcrumbs

SERVES 2 TO 4

3 tablespoons olive oil
¾ cup coarse fresh breadcrumbs
    (see page 182)
Salt
2 cloves garlic, coarsely chopped
1 large bunch kale (about 12 ounces),
    stemmed and torn into bite-size pieces

5 ounces baby spinach
4 eggs
3 tablespoons sherry vinegar or
    red wine vinegar
Freshly ground black pepper
Plain yogurt, for garnish (optional)
Hot sauce, for garnish (optional)

Preheat the oven to 325°F.

In a wide, oven-safe skillet, heat 1½ tablespoons of the oil over medium-low heat. Add the breadcrumbs and cook, stirring frequently, for about 5 minutes, until they darken a few shades and turn crisp. Transfer to a plate or bowl and season with salt.

Wipe out the skillet, return it to the heat, and add the remaining 1½ tablespoons oil. Stir in the garlic, and when fragrant, pile in the kale. Cook for 15 to 20 minutes, stirring every now and then, until wilted down and very soft and dark green. Add the spinach and cook for a few minutes more, until wilted down with the kale. Season with salt.

Raise the heat slightly and spread the kale in an even layer. Crack the eggs over the kale—you may want to crack them into a small bowl first, if you're not confident of keeping the yolks intact. Drizzle the vinegar all over, cover evenly with the breadcrumbs, and add a few grinds of black pepper. Transfer to the oven and cook until the whites are set and the yolks are cooked to your liking, 4 to 7 minutes. Serve immediately, dolloping each serving with a spoonful of yogurt and a few shakes of hot sauce, if desired.

This was originally conceived as a post–cocktail party meal to quickly throw together and soak up that extra cocktail I may have had. But it has endured, not just because it comes together so quickly, but because it tastes so much more special than a quick salad of a few ingredients should. Different types of bread can be used to make the fried croutons—my top choice is a pliant sourdough, but I've also had success with a seeded multi-grain loaf—just make sure it's one that you like the taste and texture of. And the runny yolk of the fried egg is an important component; it coats the salad leaves, functioning as dressing and adding necessary richness to balance the kimchi.

Solo Spinach Salad of Fried Egg, Kimchi, and Cheddar

SERVES 1

2 big handfuls baby spinach
¼ cup grated sharp cheddar cheese
½ cup drained, chopped Napa cabbage
    kimchi
2 teaspoons kimchi brine
    (see note on page 117)

2 tablespoons olive oil, divided
1 slice good-quality bread, torn into
    bite-size pieces
Salt
1 egg
Freshly ground black pepper

Toss the spinach, cheese, kimchi, and kimchi brine in a medium bowl.

Warm 1 tablespoon of the oil in a small skillet over medium heat. Add the bread, sprinkle with a pinch of salt, and cook, tossing periodically, until lightly browned, 3 to 4 minutes. Add to the salad.

Return the skillet to the heat and add the remaining 1 tablespoon oil. Lower the heat slightly, crack in the egg, and season with salt and black pepper. Cook until the white is set and crisp around the edges and the yolk is cooked to your liking (but still a bit runny). Immediately add the egg to the salad, plus any oil from the pan, and toss, breaking up the egg as you go. The greens will warm and just barely start to wilt. Add a few grinds of black pepper and serve immediately.

If you eat a lot of eggs but haven't yet made frittatas part of your regular routine, here's an opportunity to change that. And this is something I particularly love my small (6-inch) skillet for—for a standard 10-inch skillet, you want to triple the recipe. This formula is a reliable one: a base of sweated alliums, and then for fillings look to your leftovers—including the basic building blocks of the recipes in this book, listed below.

Anything Frittata

MAKES ONE 6-INCH FRITTATA (TO SERVE 2)

4 eggs

Olive oil

Alliums: 1 small diced onion; 3 or 4 sliced scallions; 2 minced shallots; or 1 minced leek, white and pale green parts only

Salt

About 1 scant cup cooked bulky vegetables and/or grains: wilted or marinated greens (page 54), roasted squash (page 16) or broccoli or cauliflower (page 192), sautéed or roasted mushrooms (page 136), burst cherry tomatoes, blanched or roasted asparagus, salted summer squash, leftover rice or other cooked grains

Enrichments: about ¼ cup finely grated hard cheese; crumbled feta or goat cheese; coarsely grated or cubed nicely melting cheese such as Gruyère, fontina, or cheddar; dollops of ricotta

Finishing accents: soft fresh herbs, spice blends, infused oils, flavorful sauces such as herb salsa, pesto, hot sauce, or salted yogurt

Preheat the oven to 350°F.

Crack the eggs into a bowl, add a splash of olive oil, and use a fork to whisk until combined.

Warm a 6-inch skillet over medium heat. Add a splash of olive oil, and then the alliums and a pinch of salt. Cook until softened—you don't want any raw bite left, as that will carry through in the finished frittata. Scallions will cook quickly, and onions and leeks will take the longest to get tender, so taste as you go. Scrape the onion mixture into the bowl with the eggs and stir to combine. Fold the bulky cooked vegetables and/or grains into the eggs, followed by the cheese (except if using ricotta) and chopped fresh herbs.

Return the skillet to the heat, raising it to medium-high. Add enough oil to coat the base of the skillet and swirl the pan to grease the sides. Scrape in the egg mixture. The eggs should immediately start to bubble and firm up around the edges. Use a rubber spatula to tuck under an edge and lift it, and as you do so, tilt the pan to let the uncooked egg flow underneath. Continue doing this for 2 to 3 minutes, working your way around the pan, until most of the outer edge of the frittata is set. If adding ricotta, remove the pan from the heat, then dollop the cheese over the surface.

Transfer the pan to the oven and cook until just set in the center, 8 to 12 minutes. Let cool in the pan for 5 to 10 minutes. Run a spatula around the frittata to loosen the edges, and then carefully slide it onto a plate. Serve hot, warm, or at room temperature, garnished with any finishing accents you please.

Egg on Toast

An egg on toast is a perfect solo meal because it's easy, satisfying, and indulgent sustenance. In the following recipes, I celebrate its perfect simplicity by adding a dose of vegetables. And the quality of bread here, as with all toast, makes a difference. When I buy a good loaf, I slice it, pack it up in a resealable bag, and keep it in the freezer for meals such as these; it will defrost in the toaster.

TOAST WITH SEARED SCALLIONS, ASPARAGUS COINS, AND EGG

MAKES 1 TOAST

This utilizes a trick by the celebrated science-minded food writer Harold McGee that creates less asparagus waste—there can be a lot when you go by the method of snapping the spears in half and letting the fracture point determine where the vegetable gets stringy. By slicing the stalks into thin coins, the more fibrous base of the vegetable won't be a textural issue. And scallions are a natural partner to asparagus—they're both spring vegetables, exemplifying the "what grows together goes together" axiom, but also draw out each other's sweetness when combined.

1 tablespoon butter

2 thin scallions, green and white parts, trimmed and cut into 2- or 3-inch lengths

Salt

2 thick or 5 thin asparagus stalks, pale ends trimmed off (but don't snap them), sliced into thin coins

1 thick slice bread

1 fried or poached egg

In a small skillet, melt ½ tablespoon of the butter over medium-high heat. Add the scallions and a pinch of salt. Cook until they caramelize slightly and soften, 5 to 7 minutes. Transfer to a cutting board and, when safe to handle, coarsely chop them.

Return the skillet to the heat and add a bit more of the butter, then the asparagus and a pinch of salt. Cook until just tender, 2 to 4 minutes. Add the scallions to the pan and stir to combine.

Toast the bread until well crisped, then spread with remaining butter. Pile the asparagus-scallion mixture over it, then top with the egg. Serve immediately, with knife and fork.

TOAST WITH BROILER-BLISTERED TOMATOES, PESTO, AND EGG

MAKES 1 TOAST

A quick run under the broiler isn't a hack to slow-roasting tomatoes, but it does change the flavor of fresh tomatoes and turns them into something a bit spreadable, so you get a bit of both worlds. They blister up and caramelize slightly, lending cooked notes, but retain their fresh juiciness. As you spoon them over toast, you mash them up a bit, and the juices soak into the bread. For a more savory and umami-rich flavor profile, substitute olive tapenade for the pesto here.

6 cherry tomatoes

Olive oil

Salt

1 thick slice bread

About 2 teaspoons pesto, homemade (recipe follows) or store-bought

1 fried or poached egg

Preheat the broiler or set the oven to its highest temperature, and place the rack close to the heat source.

In a small skillet or other oven-safe dish, combine the tomatoes with a bit of olive oil and a pinch of salt. Place in the broiler (or oven) and cook for 5 to 8 minutes, until the skins blister and the tomatoes start to pop.

Toast the bread until well crisped. Spread with the pesto, then spoon the tomatoes and juices over the top, mashing them a bit (be careful of tomato-juice spurts). Top with the egg, then serve immediately, with a knife and fork.

Pesto

MAKES ABOUT 1 CUP

1 small clove garlic

Salt

3 tablespoons toasted nuts (pine nuts, walnuts, almonds, hazelnuts, pecans)

2 cups stemmed, leafy herbs (basil, parsley, mint)

2 to 4 tablespoons olive oil

2 tablespoons finely grated Parmesan cheese (optional)

To make the pesto in a mortar and pestle: Pound together the garlic and a pinch of salt until you have a paste. Add the nuts and pound them—well, not so much pounding as "tap-tap-tapping" them—into the mixture until they're finely ground. Add the herbs a handful at a time, adding more as they collapse into the mixture. Stir in the olive oil until your desired consistency is reached, then add the cheese, if using.

To make the pesto in a food processor: Combine the garlic, a pinch of salt, and the nuts in a food processor and pulse until uniformly ground. Add the herbs and pulse until they collapse and integrate into the nuts. With the motor running, stream in the olive oil until your desired consistency is reached. Stir in the cheese, if using.

TOAST WITH GARLICKY WHITE BEANS AND EGG

MAKES 1 TOAST

A poached egg on top of beans, where the runny yolk seeps into the beans, is a decadent and filling meal for breakfast, lunch, or dinner. Here, the beans are laced with tender slabs of garlic, which perfume the whole dish. If you're using canned beans and want to make use of the whole can, you can easily multiply this recipe to serve 4.

Olive oil

1 plump clove garlic, thinly sliced

About ½ cup cooked white beans
(cannellini, great northern, navy)

¼ teaspoon kosher salt

1 heaping tablespoon chopped dill
or minced chives (optional)

1 thick slice bread

1 poached egg

Flaky salt

Freshly ground black pepper

In a small saucepan or skillet, warm about 1 tablespoon olive oil over medium-low heat. Add the garlic and cook, stirring often, until soft (but not browned or crisp), 1 to 2 minutes. Add the beans and kosher salt and cook, stirring periodically, until heated through, about 5 minutes. Add 1 tablespoon water and mash some of the beans to create a bit of a saucy consistency (if too thin, allow the beans to reduce for a few minutes). Stir in the herbs, if using.

Toast the bread until well crisped, then drizzle with olive oil. Spoon the beans over the bread and top with the egg. Drizzle once more with a little olive oil, sprinkle with flaky salt and black pepper, then serve immediately, with a knife and fork.

TOAST WITH GARLICKY
WHITE BEANS AND EGG,
PAGE 129

TOAST WITH SPINACH,
SMOKED PAPRIKA OIL,
AND FRIED EGG,
PAGE 132

TOAST WITH BROILER-
BLISTERED TOMATOES,
PESTO, AND EGG,
PAGE 127

TOAST WITH SEARED
SCALLIONS, ASPARAGUS
COINS, AND EGG,
PAGE 127

TOAST WITH SPINACH, SMOKED PAPRIKA OIL, AND FRIED EGG

MAKES 1 TOAST

Blooming dried spices in warm oil is an easy way to amplify their flavor. And smoked paprika, a spice vegetarians have long loved for what some call a "meaty" flavor profile, takes well to the technique, turning the olive oil into a flavorful burnt-crimson sauce. Use any greens you like here, adjusting the cooking time as necessary.

1 thick slice bread
Olive oil
2 handfuls baby spinach (2 cups)
Salt

1 egg
¼ teaspoon smoked paprika
Freshly ground black pepper

Toast the bread until well crisped.

Warm a splash of oil in a small skillet over medium heat, then add the spinach. Cook, stirring often, until wilted, 1 to 2 minutes. Season with a pinch of salt, then spread over the toast. Return the skillet to the heat and add another splash of oil. Fry the egg to your preference, then slide it on top of the spinach. Return the skillet to the heat once more and add a final splash of oil. Stir in the paprika and cook until fragrant, 20 or 30 seconds. Drizzle over the egg. Sprinkle with salt and black pepper, then serve immediately, with a knife and fork.

CHAPTER 10

A Pile of Mushrooms

Where would vegetarians be without mushrooms? They're loved for their distinctive "meaty" texture, and I've been a big fan since I was a kid. What I find most appealing about them is their versatility. I used to like raw white mushrooms from the salad bar drenched with a creamy dressing. Then it was the buttery little slips of sautéed mushrooms that I'd make with my mom, or the whole creminis we'd sear and add to braised stews. Through learning about different Asian cuisines, I discovered how much flavor a dried mushroom can add to soups and stocks. Later, I developed an interest in cultivated versions of wild mushrooms like maitake, king trumpets, and oyster mushrooms, and grew an appreciation for the different flavors they add to a dish and different ways they take to applications of heat.

In recent years, many health experts have declared mushrooms a superfood. They are reported to be rich in key antioxidants that support healthy aging, and they're also a good source of plant-based protein and have the highest concentration of vitamin D of any non-meat food. This has led to an array of new products, like mushroom coffee and tea, as well as various powdered supplements. And an increasing variety of mushrooms is becoming available in the produce aisle.

I like to stock up on a few cartons of mushrooms at the supermarket, whether it's white buttons or creminis, shiitakes, or a medley of different "wild" mushrooms (such as oysters, king trumpets, and chanterelles; they are usually cultivated, even if marketed as wild). Your local farmers market may have a mushroom forager who sells truly wild mushrooms or a mushroom purveyor who cultivates rarer varieties in smaller amounts than commercial producers. All of them are worth seeking out.

At home I'll take them in a number of different directions, roasting off a tray to put to use throughout the week (page 136) or thinly shaving them for soups or salads (pages 142 and 148), showing off their unique texture when eaten raw. I love them, as most people do, in rich treatments like pasta (page 139) and baked stratas (page 147), but also in lighter fare such as broth bowls and in green salads. My aim is to make my love of their great versatility infectious.

Look for mushrooms that are dry and firm, that don't appear glistening with moisture. Their gills should appear healthy, not falling out, and the caps shouldn't have the appearance of a flower that's overgrown. They're best stored in the refrigerator in a paper bag or something similar that's a bit absorbent and breathable. And to wash them, you can either wipe them off with a damp cloth or plunge them into a bowl of water, give a quick shake with your fingers to dislodge any clumps of dirt, and then wrap them up in a clean towel to dry.

Roasting mushrooms rather than sautéing them results in fungi that are a bit drier with a chewier texture. It's also a very hands-off method that minimizes the worry about overcrowding in the pan, preventing you from attaining that golden sear. Prepared in a large batch and packed away for future meals, roasted mushrooms are an extraordinarily useful ingredient to keep on hand—and like the marinated greens, doing the prep work upfront extends their shelf life in your fridge. You can use roasted mushrooms in many recipes throughout this book—in the stovetop lasagna (page 30), simple tostadas (page 58), or a frittata (page 125), for example. These savory mushrooms make a great side dish on their own tossed with a handful of parsley leaves, chopped chives, or a sprinkle of fresh oregano leaves.

Roasted Mushrooms

MAKES ABOUT 3 CUPS

1 pound mushrooms, any variety
   or combination
2 tablespoons olive oil

2 teaspoons red or white wine vinegar,
   or apple cider vinegar
Salt
Freshly ground black pepper

Preheat the oven to 400°F.

Trim off and discard the tough and/or unseemly stems of any mushrooms, then cut or tear the caps into roughly 1-inch pieces. Arrange on a baking sheet, grouping the different varieties (if any) together. Drizzle with the oil and vinegar and sprinkle with salt and black pepper. Use your hands to mix well to evenly coat them, then transfer to the oven and roast until tender and juicy—first they'll release a lot of liquid, then most of it cooks off, which is when they're usually done. Start checking on them after 10 minutes, tasting and testing doneness with a paring knife, allowing 15 to 20 minutes total. Delicate mushrooms like oysters will cook most quickly, and if they're part of the mix remove them with a spatula once they're cooked, then return the baking sheet to the oven and let the remaining mushroom varieties finish.

Cooled and stored in an airtight container in the fridge, they'll keep for several days.

Here the tofu functions a bit like a thick slice of cheese—you want the tofu to fit over most of the bread, so slice it off the side of the block of tofu that offers the greatest length and width, or make multiple smaller slices to create an equivalent-size piece. The sandwich has a sweet-salty flavor profile, thanks to the maple and soy sauce glaze, and plenty of textural contrast with the mushrooms, tofu, crisp lettuce, and chewy bread.

Roasted Mushroom and
Maple-Tofu Sandwich

MAKES 1 SANDWICH

Olive oil

1 wide slice firm tofu, about ½ inch thick, blotted dry

Salt

¼ cup Roasted Mushrooms (page 136), coarsely chopped

1 teaspoon soy sauce

1 teaspoon maple syrup

2 slices good sandwich bread, toasted

Egg-based mayonnaise or vegan mayo

1 or 2 pieces crisp lettuce

Warm a bit of olive oil in a small skillet (or a large one if you're multiplying the recipe) over medium-high heat, then carefully add the tofu. Sprinkle with salt and cook without disturbing for about 2 minutes, until lightly golden on the bottom. Flip and repeat. Add the mushrooms to the pan, then pour the soy sauce and maple syrup over everything. Cook, nudging things around a bit, until the liquid thickens and the mushrooms are heated through, about 2 minutes, then remove from the heat.

Spread a thin layer of mayo over each slice of bread. Place the tofu slab and mushrooms over one slice. Top with the lettuce, close the sandwich with the reserved slice, then cut in half and serve hot.

If you've ever opened up a box of lasagna noodles to discover it's filled with shards and chipped slabs of pasta, this is the dish for you (though you can substitute another flat and "forkable" pasta you have on hand). I love all the texture here: big chunks of roasted mushrooms, crunchy walnuts, irregular-size noodles, and creamy, rich ricotta. A mild-flavored, nut-based "ricotta" is a fine substitute, and if you swap olive oil for the butter and use a vegan pesto, you'll have a winning vegan pasta.

Broken Pasta with Roasted Mushrooms, Caramelized Onions, Walnuts, and Pesto'd Ricotta

SERVES 4

2 tablespoons butter
1 onion, sliced into thin strips
2 cloves garlic, sliced
½ teaspoon salt, plus more for cooking the pasta
¼ teaspoon red pepper flakes
2 teaspoons red wine vinegar
1½ cups Roasted Mushrooms (page 136)
¼ cup ricotta cheese

2 tablespoons store-bought or homemade pesto (page 128)
8 ounces lasagna noodles or other flat, "forkable" medium-size pasta shape
¾ cup toasted walnuts, coarsely chopped or crushed
1 cup whole parsley leaves
Lemon zest
Freshly ground black pepper

In a wide skillet or Dutch oven, melt the butter over medium heat. When the foaming subsides, add the onion, garlic, salt, and red pepper flakes. Stir to coat the onions, then cook without disturbing for 5 minutes or so, until the onions take on some color on the bottom. Stir, then cook undisturbed again for 5 minutes. Repeat this process until the onions are caramelized and sweet, 20 to 25 minutes, then deglaze with the vinegar. Stir in the mushrooms and remove from the heat.

In a small bowl, mix together the ricotta and pesto.

Meanwhile, bring a pot of water to a rolling boil and salt it well. Working a small stack at a time, break the lasagna noodles over the pot into irregular-size pieces, dropping them directly into the water, and cook until tender, using the package instructions as a guide. Reserve a few ladlesful of the pasta cooking water, then strain the noodles and add them directly to the pot with the mushrooms.

Stir to combine, loosening with some of the reserved water as needed. Stir in the walnuts, parsley, and several swipes of lemon zest, then serve immediately, dolloping each serving with the ricotta-pesto mixture, a dusting of black pepper, and pinches of additional salt, if needed, at the table.

A Pile of Mushrooms

Summer rolls—in which an assortment of vegetables and herbs and other fillings are wrapped up in a reconstituted rice paper sheet (they're not deep fried as spring rolls sometimes are)—can be a therapeutic cooking project if you steel yourself for patience at the outset. For me, it usually takes one or two before I find my groove and figure out how to work with the rice paper. But once you have them made, they're perfect travel food. Wrap them in moist paper towels and line them up in an airtight container and they'll keep for a few hours.

Wintertime Summer Rolls with Roasted Mushrooms and Citrus

SERVES 4

Summer rolls

2 oranges

8 large rice paper wrappers

1 bunch basil or mint

1 cup Roasted Mushrooms (page 136), coarsely chopped

1 medium carrot, shredded

1 cucumber, sliced into long, thin spears

3 scallions, green and white parts, thinly sliced

Dipping sauce

2 tablespoons soy sauce

1 tablespoon fresh lime juice

1 tablespoon apple cider vinegar

1 teaspoon honey

Prepare the oranges: Trim off the top and bottom ends, then cut off all the peel and pith. Holding the peeled fruit in your hand over a bowl to collect the juices, trim the fruit free of its membranes. Add the citrus supremes to the bowl with the juice.

Fill a shallow pan with warm water. Lay a clean kitchen cloth over a work surface. Arrange the remaining summer roll ingredients so they're within easy reach.

To make each roll: Dip a rice paper wrapper in the warm water and soak for about 10 seconds, just until pliable. Remove from the water and lay it over the kitchen towel. On the bottom third of the roll, arrange a few mint leaves in a little strip. Top with about one-eighth of the mushrooms, carrot, cucumber, scallions, and citrus supremes. Fold the left and right edges over the filling, then roll up like a burrito. Transfer to a plate or baking sheet and cover loosely with a lightly moistened clean kitchen towel, and repeat with remaining rice paper wrappers until you have 8 summer rolls. Chill in the refrigerator.

To make the dipping sauce, whisk together all the ingredients until combined.

Slice the summer rolls in half diagonally and serve with the dipping sauce on the side.

This recipe is a spin on the polenta with beans on page 78, except that here it's drizzled with cream and baked, creating a bubbling, bronzed topping that'll warm you on a cold night. Adding a half cup or so of chopped wilted greens—or the Marinated Greens on page 54—along with the mushrooms adds some color, texture, and an extra dose of vegetables. In my experience, there isn't a great vegan substitute for the cream, as the cream moistens and enriches the dish and gives it a glaze, but you can most certainly omit the cream and instead drizzle the assembled mushrooms and polenta with a bit of extra olive oil before baking. It will be bubbling and lightly browned when pulled out of the oven.

Roasted Mushroom Polenta Bake

SERVES 4

1 teaspoon salt
1 cup polenta
2 tablespoons olive oil
2 cups Roasted Mushrooms (page 136)

2 teaspoons thyme leaves, or
  ½ teaspoon dried thyme
2 tablespoons heavy cream

Preheat the oven to 375°F.

In a medium saucepan, bring 4 cups water to a boil, then reduce to a simmer and add ½ teaspoon of the salt. While whisking, sprinkle in the polenta and keep whisking until the polenta incorporates into the liquid (rather than sinks to the bottom), 2 to 3 minutes. Reduce the heat to the lowest setting and simmer uncovered, whisking periodically to prevent the bottom from scorching, until the polenta is thick and the grains are tender, 15 to 20 minutes. Make sure to taste as you go, using caution, as it's very hot right out of the pot. Whisk in the olive oil, then pour into a 2-quart baking dish.

Scatter the mushrooms and the thyme over the polenta, then drizzle with the cream. Transfer to the oven and cook for about 15 minutes, until bubbling along the edges. Sprinkle with remaining salt and serve hot.

I love this fragrant, savory broth, and when I make it, I always set aside a mugful for sipping. It's a rejuvenating elixir, exactly the sort of thing I crave when I'm warding off a cold. In this brothy soup, thinly sliced raw mushrooms are the last thing to go in. The broth just barely cooks them, but for the most part it showcases the mushrooms in their raw state, with their earthy flavor and lightly spongy texture. To save a pot at the stove, you can prepare the broth up to a day in advance and then reheat it in the microwave.

Miso Soba Bowl with Greens and Mushrooms

SERVES 4

Olive oil

1 medium onion, peeled and halved
   through the stem

3 cloves garlic, smashed

2-inch piece ginger, peeled and
   coarsely chopped

6 cremini or button mushrooms,
   stems and caps separated

2 tablespoons miso paste

Salt

One 9.5-ounce package soba noodles

1 package silken tofu (about 12 ounces),
   cut into small cubes

2 cups tender greens (baby spinach,
   baby kale, blends of Asian greens)

2 scallions, green and white parts,
   thinly sliced

Prepare the broth: In a medium saucepan set over medium-high heat, heat a splash of olive oil. Add the onion, cut-side down, and cook until well colored on the bottom, 5 to 7 minutes. Add the garlic, ginger, mushroom caps, and 6 cups water. Bring to a boil, then turn the heat down to a gentle simmer and cook for 20 minutes. Strain out the solids using a cheesecloth-lined colander or a fine-mesh sieve and return the broth to the pot.

In a small bowl, whisk together a ladleful of the broth with the miso paste to dilute it, then pour this into the pot along with ¾ teaspoon salt. Taste for seasoning. Before assembling the bowls, make sure the broth is hot.

Bring a saucepan of salted water to a boil and add the soba noodles. Cook until just tender, using the package instructions as a guide, then immediately drain and rinse with cold water. Drain well, then divide among 4 bowls.

Thinly slice the mushroom caps, either with a mandoline or sharp chef's knife, then scatter them over the noodles along with the tofu and greens. Ladle the piping-hot broth over everything. Garnish with the scallions and serve immediately.

Shiitake mushrooms, more so than other mushroom varieties, hold onto their chewy texture once cooked, which means that they are a great choice for lending some texture to a dish, as they do here. In these crisp lettuce cups, mushrooms mingle with the flavors of miso, soy, and tahini to create an umami-rich bite that is a perfect appetizer or side dish.

Shiitake Lettuce Cups

SERVES 4 AS A SIDE

7 ounces shiitake mushrooms,
    stems trimmed and discarded
1 tablespoon olive oil
4 scallions, green and white parts,
    sliced into ¼-inch segments
1 teaspoon soy sauce
1 teaspoon rice vinegar or
    apple cider vinegar
1 teaspoon toasted sesame oil

¼ teaspoon salt
Freshly ground black pepper
Fresh lime juice
2 tablespoons tahini
1 tablespoon miso paste
1 scant teaspoon maple syrup
12 leaves from hearts of romaine, or
    other crisp lettuce cups

Thinly slice the shiitake caps. Warm the oil over medium-high heat, then add the mushrooms and cook until juicy and tender, stirring every now and then so that they sear and caramelize a bit, 5 to 7 minutes. Stir in the scallions, then deglaze with the soy sauce and vinegar, scraping up any browned bits from the bottom of the pan. Remove from the heat and add the sesame oil, salt, a few grinds of black pepper, and lime juice to taste.

Meanwhile, in a small bowl, stir together the tahini, miso, and maple syrup.

To assemble, add a little smear of the tahini-miso paste to the lettuce leaves (it's quite flavorful, so you don't need much), then divide the warm mushrooms on top. Serve while the mushrooms are still warm or at room temperature.

Here's an uncompromisingly flavorful pasta dish that contains no cheese or dairy, though a poached egg on top wouldn't be a bad idea. Radicchio is one of my favorite vegetables, especially when it's cooked. It sheds some of its bitterness and becomes a bit smoky, pairing gorgeously with the nuts and mushrooms as it collapses and mingles with the pasta. This pasta dish also has almost a one-to-one ratio of pasta to fillings, which is a good thing if you love these fillings as much as I do.

Mushroom and Radicchio Pasta with Nutty Gremolata

SERVES 2

Salt

6 ounces rombi, bowties, broken lasagna noodles, or other flat, small noodle shapes

1 small clove garlic, peeled

¼ cup toasted hazelnuts, almonds, or walnuts

½ teaspoon lemon zest

Olive oil

6 ounces mushrooms, ideally a combination, sliced or torn into uniform sizes

2 shallots, diced

½ medium head radicchio, chopped

Freshly ground black pepper

Bring a pot of well-salted water to boil—it should taste like seawater. Add the pasta and cook until tender, using the package instructions as a guide. Reserve a cupful of the cooking water, then drain the pasta.

To make the gremolata, in a mortar and pestle, or on the cutting board, pound (or chop) the garlic with a big pinch of salt until you have a paste. Add the nuts and lemon zest and pound (or chop) until finely ground—just before it becomes a paste.

Meanwhile, heat a thin layer of olive oil in a wide skillet or Dutch oven over medium-high heat and sear the mushrooms. Cook them in batches by variety, as they all have different cooking times, anywhere from 2 to 5 minutes per side. Transfer to a plate and season with salt. Reduce the heat to medium and add another splash of oil to the pan, followed by the shallots. Cook until they begin to soften, 2 to 3 minutes, then stir in the radicchio and a few pinches of salt. Cook until collapsed and flavorful, about 10 minutes, and taste for seasoning. Stir in the mushrooms, then the cooked pasta. Toss, adding splashes of the pasta cooking water as needed to loosen the pasta. Stir in the gremolata. Top with several grinds of black pepper and serve immediately.

This brunch dish is inspired by the sausage strata my family has always made for Christmas morning. The mushrooms, ground or finely chopped and then cooked down to a concentrated, earthy paste, look a bit like the sausage in my family's recipe when they're folded into the eggs. You can assemble this the night before and then bake it off in the morning. If you have day-old bread, skip the drying step. And as far as bread goes, don't choose a loaf that's dense or heavy—you want something airy and with a light crumb, like a French boule or Italian ciabatta. Sear leftover slabs in a bit of olive oil or butter for a snack.

Skillet Mushroom Strata

SERVES 6

6 cups airy bread, torn or cut into
  bite-size pieces (12 ounces)
5 eggs
1 cup whole milk or unflavored
  nondairy milk
2 tablespoons olive oil, plus more for
  greasing

1 teaspoon salt, divided
1 pound cremini or button mushrooms
2 tablespoons butter or olive oil
½ teaspoon dried sage
Pinch red pepper flakes
2 ounces goat cheese or feta cheese,
  crumbled

Preheat the oven to 300°F.

Spread the bread out on a baking sheet and bake for 15 minutes, or until slightly dried out and lightly crisp. (Skip this step if your bread is already day-old and slightly dried out.)

Raise the oven temperature to 375°F.

Beat the eggs, milk, olive oil, and ½ teaspoon of the salt in a large bowl until combined. Add the toasted bread, folding with a spatula until well coated. Set aside for 15 to 20 minutes as you prepare the mushrooms so the bread has time to soak up the egg mixture.

Place the mushrooms in a food processor and pulse until ground to about the size of small peas, in batches if necessary (or, if you don't have a food processor, finely dice by hand—it can be a meditative task). Melt the butter in a deep skillet over medium heat, then add the mushrooms, the remaining ½ teaspoon salt, the sage, and the red pepper flakes. Cook, stirring every now and then, until the mushrooms are reduced and a little sludgy looking and the pan is dry—they'll first soak up the oil, then release their water, and then once the water cooks off they're ready, 12 to 15 minutes.

Scrape the mushroom mixture into the bowl with the bread and eggs and fold just until the mushrooms are mostly distributed. Wipe out the skillet, brush lightly with oil, then press the bread mixture into the pan. Sprinkle the cheese evenly over the top. Transfer to the oven and bake until a tester comes out clean, about 30 minutes. Serve warm or at room temperature.

A Pile of Mushrooms

I've been a fan of raw mushrooms since I was a kid, so I've been happy to see them making a comeback at New York restaurants in the past few years. I've always liked their quiet but fresh flavor and their springy bounce. In this salad, the color palette—pale whites and browns—may leave something to be desired, but the gorgeous medley of textures and very complementary flavors makes up for it. This is an attractive one to serve for a dinner party.

Shaved Mushroom, Celery, and Sesame Salad

SERVES 4

2 stalks celery, ends trimmed
5 ounces cremini or button mushrooms
   (about 8), ends trimmed
1½ teaspoons fresh lemon juice
1½ teaspoons white wine vinegar
Kosher salt

2 tablespoons well-stirred tahini
1 tablespoon olive oil
Handful whole parsley leaves
Flaky salt
Freshly ground black pepper

To de-string the celery, make a small cut into the outer base end of the celery stalk, no more than ⅛-inch deep, and pull along the length of the stalk. If it's a wide stalk, repeat, working around the outer edge, until no more strings are released. Using a mandoline, cut the celery and mushrooms into paper-thin shavings. In a large bowl, combine the celery and mushrooms and toss with the lemon juice, vinegar, and ½ teaspoon kosher salt and let stand for 5 minutes.

Meanwhile, stir together the tahini and about 2 tablespoons water in a small bowl until smooth. Don't fret if it looks dry and lumpy; just keep stirring. The consistency should be about that of whipped cream cheese; adjust as needed by adding a bit more water or a bit more tahini. Season with a pinch of kosher salt, then using the back of a spoon, smear the mixture over your serving platter or bowl or divide it among 4 salad plates.

Add the olive oil and parsley to the mushrooms and gently toss to combine, then pile on top of the tahini. Sprinkle with a few pinches of flaky salt and a few grinds of black pepper.

Serve immediately, making sure to scrape up the tahini smear along with the mushroom-celery salad. Eat within an hour or so, as the mushrooms start releasing liquid as the salad sits.

This salad doesn't sound like much, but its simplicity belies the magic of textures, temperatures, and flavors it contains. I serve it for friends to wild acclaim. Peppery arugula is my favorite salad green to use here, but any spicy green you've got will work: watercress, mizuna, or an Asian green like tatsoi. And it's a nice way to showcase a variety of good mushrooms. Use one of those "chef sampler packs" available at lots of supermarkets.

Warm Arugula Salad with Seared Mushrooms and Parmesan

SERVES 4

8 ounces mixed mushrooms: cremini, oyster, king trumpet, shiitake, trimmed and/or stemmed if necessary
Olive oil
¼ teaspoon salt, plus more for cooking the mushrooms
Freshly ground black pepper

2 tablespoons red wine vinegar
1 heaping teaspoon Dijon mustard
1 clove garlic, smashed
4 handfuls baby arugula or other spicy salad green
Parmesan or pecorino cheese

Cut or tear the mushrooms into large bite-size pieces. Warm a splash of olive oil in a skillet over medium-high heat. Working in batches, add as many mushrooms as will fit in a comfortable single layer and cook undisturbed until, after a few minutes, they take on some color. Flip and repeat. Continue cooking until the mushrooms are seared, tender, and juicy, usually 2 to 5 minutes per side, transferring them to a plate as they finish cooking, as different varieties will have different cooking times. Season with salt and black pepper.

Meanwhile, whisk together the vinegar, mustard, and ¼ teaspoon salt in a small bowl.

Reduce the heat to medium-low and add all the cooked mushrooms back to the skillet, then add the garlic. Pour the vinegar mixture over the mushrooms and quickly (but gently) stir to coat as the liquid bubbles away. Remove the pan from the heat and pick out the garlic.

Pile the arugula on top and drizzle with about 2 tablespoons olive oil. Toss the greens with the mushrooms for about 15 seconds, until they just start to wilt, then immediately divide among 4 serving plates. Grate cheese over the top or make shavings using a vegetable peeler. Add a few grinds of black pepper, then serve.

CHAPTER 11

A Stack of Tortillas

As a kid, my after-school snack was what my brother and I called a "cheese tortilla": a commercially made flour tortilla strewn with grated cheddar, microwaved, and rolled up, usually dripping grease out the end as we ate. As I got older, I became aware of this as a not-very-nourishing snack (though they're no doubt delicious), and so they got moved out of rotation in favor of healthy ones. Compared to the soft goo that I favored growing up, corn tortillas always seemed a little dry and brittle by comparison.

But I warmed up to them, and with my evolving palate and developing appreciation for Mexican food came a new fondness for the complexity, nuance, and noble texture of good corn tortillas. I also came to learn that what passes for tortillas in the United States is often kind of an embarrassment. Grocery store aisles are end-capped with stacks of tortillas that seem to have a shelf life of eternity and an alarming list of ingredients.

Given the long, long tradition of tortilla making in Mexico, Central America, and South America, I've learned to see tortillas as I do bread: best when they're fresh and locally made. Regions have their own local tortilla producers (and in the US they're often harder to find than bread bakeries), and it's worthwhile to search for tortillas that are made near where you live. But I will pick up national brands at the grocery store, and when I do, I go by the ingredient list. Proper corn tortillas should contain just masa harina (dried corn and lime) and salt. Commercial tortillas often have lots of other things added, including preservatives to extend that aforementioned shelf life, wheat gluten and gums to soften the texture, and sugar or high-fructose corn syrup to sweeten them.

But once I have tortillas in my kitchen, as I usually do now, they are just the thing to spark an idea for dinner. I'm less inclined to blanket them in cheese as I once was, and instead I find inspiration in vegetables: greens, mushrooms, winter and summer squash, beans, peppers—all of these make delicious taco fillings. Sometimes I'll make a refreshing limey salad when I happen to have some ripe summer fruit or a vegetable-forward dish of enchiladas drenched in a smoky-sweet red sauce. I've never found a vegetable that didn't taste good on a tortilla in some way, so it surprises me how limited vegetarian options still are in Mexican restaurants here in the United States.

A final note: If eating corn tortillas out of hand, they must be warmed. This can be done in a number of ways. You can char them over the flame of a gas burner or a grill. You can brush them lightly with water and place them in a skillet set over a moderate flame, flipping them over a few times until warmed and pliant. Or you can wrap them up in a moist towel and leave them in a low oven for 15 to 20 minutes, which I find to be the best method when you're serving a crowd.

A Few Vegetable Tacos

Vegetarian tacos are ripe with potential: as a way to showcase peak-season produce, to round out a smattering of leftovers into something more substantial, and as a festive centerpiece to a gathering. Here are a few of my favorites, which employ what I think are fun techniques for getting the most flavor out of different vegetables.

BRAISED PORTOBELLO TACOS

SERVES 4

While Roasted Mushrooms (page 136) work very well in tacos, I love this braising method, which I first learned about in the Rancho Gordo newsletter. It's similar, vaguely, to the way traditional carnitas are made: simmered in water so as to stay moist, and then left to sizzle in the fat that remains. They fit very snugly inside a tortilla this way and are excellent with a little smear of spicy mayo.

2 tablespoons butter or olive oil

1 tablespoon tomato paste

½ teaspoon ground cumin

½ teaspoon dried oregano

6 portobello mushrooms, gills scraped out with a spoon, sliced into ¼-inch-thick strips

Salt

½ cup thinly sliced red onion

2 tablespoons red or white wine vinegar, or apple cider vinegar

¼ cup mayonnaise

1 tablespoon sriracha or dashes of hot sauce

8 tortillas, warmed just before serving (see page 153)

Lime wedges

Melt the butter or warm the oil in a Dutch oven or other large saucepan over medium heat, then stir in the tomato paste, cumin, and oregano. Pile in the sliced mushrooms and add ½ teaspoon salt and ¾ cup water. Stir gently a few times to combine. Bring to a rapid simmer, partially cover, and cook for 10 to 15 minutes, until most the water has cooked off. Remove the lid and continue cooking until the mushrooms are quite reduced and frying in the almost-dry pan.

Meanwhile, combine the sliced onion with a few pinches of salt in a small bowl, mixing with your fingers to combine. Add the vinegar and let stand for at least 10 minutes; the onions can be made in advance and will keep for several days in an airtight container in the refrigerator. In another small bowl, stir together the mayonnaise and sriracha; taste and add more heat if you'd like.

To serve, spoon the braised mushrooms on a warmed tortilla, top with a dollop of the spiced mayo and a little pile of pickled onions, and finish with a spritz of lime.

BEAN TACOS WITH
LIME SLAW, PAGE 161

CREAMED POBLANO
TACOS, PAGE 160

BREAKFAST TACOS,
PAGE 159

SALAD TACOS,
PAGE 158

BRAISED
PORTOBELLO TACOS,
PAGE 155

SALAD TACOS

I first encountered this ingeniousness in Alice Waters's book *My Pantry*. These tacos are the perfect snack or light lunch, and the principle is so straightforward it hardly merits a recipe: Take your favorite green salad and fold it up in a warm tortilla. Which is one way of saying, too, that this recipe, without the tortillas, is one of my favorite green salads.

2 shallots, cut into thin rings

¼ teaspoon salt

Pinch sugar

¼ cup red wine vinegar

4 cups tender and/or crunchy salad greens

2 tablespoons olive oil

Salt

Freshly ground black pepper

1 ripe avocado

8 corn tortillas, warmed just before serving (see page 153)

Additional toppings: toasted nuts or seeds, crumbled goat cheese, sliced radishes

Combine the shallots, salt, and sugar in a small bowl and rub them with your fingers until glistening. Add the vinegar and let stand for about 15 minutes.

Place the greens in a large bowl. Lift the pickled shallots out of their liquid, reserving it, and add them to the greens. Toss the salad with about 2 teaspoons of the pickling liquid, the olive oil, a pinch of salt, and a few grinds of black pepper.

Cut the avocado into eighths. For each taco, mash an avocado wedge onto a warm tortilla, sprinkle it with a pinch of salt, then fill with the dressed greens and any other toppings of choice, and serve.

BREAKFAST TACOS

SERVES 4

There are lots of ways to make breakfast tacos, but I always come back to the simplest one, with potatoes, scallions, eggs, and cheddar cheese. You want to use small new potatoes here—each one about the size of a ping-pong ball. If you use another potato, slice it into a similarly small and thin size. This filling works just as well rolled into warmed flour tortillas, in which case you'll have breakfast burritos.

2 tablespoons olive oil or butter

8 small waxy potatoes (about 3 ounces total), sliced into thin discs

Salt

4 scallions, green and white parts, thinly sliced

6 eggs, lightly beaten

⅔ cup grated cheddar or other sharp, nicely melting cheese

8 corn tortillas, warmed just before serving (see page 153)

Avocado wedges (optional)

Handful cilantro leaves (optional)

Hot sauce or salsa, for the table

Warm the oil or melt the butter in a medium skillet over medium heat. Add the potatoes, arranging them in a single layer as best as you can manage, and cook until browned on the bottom, about 5 minutes. Flip and repeat on the other side and sprinkle with salt. Add 3 tablespoons water to the pan, cover, and cook for about 3 minutes—this will finish cooking the potatoes by steaming them. Test for doneness with a paring knife, ensuring that all the pieces are cooked thoroughly.

Add the scallions and cook for another minute or so, until they soften. Lower the heat and allow the pan to cool a bit, then pour in the eggs and scramble them with the potatoes until just set, about 3 to 4 minutes. Stir in the cheese, then divide the eggs among the warm tortillas, top with avocado wedges and a few cilantro leaves, if using, and splashes of hot sauce, and serve immediately.

CREAMED POBLANO TACOS

SERVES 4

This is essentially *rajas con crema*, a classic Mexican dish that's often served as a side or in tortillas. If for some reason you can't find poblanos, bell peppers make a good substitute. You'll use the gas flame of a stovetop burner to char-roast them, a technique that works well for roasting any kind of pepper (including in the jalapeño relish on page 169), and even eggplants. But if you don't have a gas stove, you can roast the peppers under the broiler, rotating them every minute or two until charred all over, or on the grill. This latter method has the advantage of enabling you to cook all the peppers at once.

4 poblano or bell peppers

Olive oil

1 onion, cut into strips

2 cloves garlic, sliced

½ cup dairy cream or nondairy cream, such as cashew cream

Salt

8 small corn tortillas, warmed just before serving (see page 153)

¼ cup cilantro sprigs

Lime wedges

Using metal tongs, place the peppers directly over the flame of a gas burner set on high. Cook the peppers, turning them periodically, until blackened all over, 4 to 10 minutes. Place them in a bowl and cover with plastic wrap, sealing tightly, to let them steam for about 10 minutes. When safe to handle, rub off the skins and remove the seeds and ribs, then cut or tear the flesh into thick strips.

Heat a splash of oil in a medium skillet over medium heat. Add the onion and garlic and cook until they are softened, 6 to 8 minutes. Stir in the peppers, then pour in the cream. Bring to a gentle simmer and cook for 1 to 2 minutes, until thickened just a touch. Season with salt.

To serve, spoon the peppers and cream onto the warmed tortillas and top with the cilantro sprigs and spritzes of lime juice.

BEAN TACOS WITH LIME SLAW

SERVES 4

Any bean can be jazzed up with a bright, citrusy slaw, and this slaw employs a trick I like in which the citrus is chopped up and mixed in to add juicy little bites. I like to make these tacos with black beans or pinto beans, but any starchy bean—kidney, black-eyed pea, and so on—will do. If using home-cooked beans, use the bean broth in place of water to loosen them up.

2 tablespoons olive oil

1 teaspoon cumin seeds

1 teaspoon smoked paprika

3 cups (two 14.5-ounce cans) black beans or pinto beans, rinsed

1 tablespoon butter, optional

Salt

1 orange

2 cups shredded green or red cabbage

Juice of 1 lime

Dash cayenne

8 corn tortillas, warmed just before serving (see page 153)

Cotija, feta, or other crumbly, salty white cheese

Warm the oil in a medium skillet over medium heat. Add the cumin and paprika and stir for about 30 seconds, until fragrant, then add the rinsed beans. Pour in ½ cup water and ¾ teaspoon salt and bring to a simmer. Cook for about 10 minutes, stirring and mashing slightly with a spatula or wooden spoon. The beans should not be soupy or pasty; adjust the consistency with water or by cooking for a few minutes longer as needed. It will thicken as it sits. Just before serving, stir in the butter, if using, and season with salt.

Prepare the orange: Trim off the top and bottom ends, then cut off all the peel and pith. Holding the peeled fruit in your hand over a bowl to collect the juices, trim the fruit free of its membranes. Add the citrus supremes to the bowl with the juice.

Add the cabbage, lime juice, cayenne, and ¼ teaspoon salt to the bowl with the orange and let stand for 10 to 15 minutes to soften a bit. Taste and adjust seasoning as necessary.

To serve, spoon the warm beans onto a tortilla and top with a bit of slaw and a sprinkle of cheese.

As a bitter green, broccoli rabe is one of those vegetables that takes well to creamy and rich ingredients like cheese—and therefore works great in quesadillas. When I make a quesadilla for just myself, I usually just cook it in a lightly oiled skillet, but when feeding a crowd, baking them, as instructed in this recipe, is a big time-saver. And the salsa comes together in the time it takes to assemble the quesadillas, but feel free to sub a favorite smooth-textured store-bought one.

Baked Broccoli Rabe Quesadillas with Roasted Tomato Salsa

MAKES 6 QUESADILLAS

1 bunch broccoli rabe, tough stems trimmed and discarded
3 scallions, green and white parts, thinly sliced
Olive oil
Juice of ½ lime
Salt

One 15-ounce can black beans, rinsed
12 corn tortillas
Roasted Tomato Salsa (recipe follows) or comparable store-bought salsa
1½ cups grated Monterey Jack cheese
Sour cream, for serving

Preheat the oven to 375°F.

Bring ½ inch water to a boil in a medium saucepan. Add the broccoli rabe and steam until the leaves are collapsed and the thick stems are tender, 3 to 5 minutes. Drain in a colander, pressing gently to extract as much water as possible. When cool enough to handle, transfer to a cutting board and coarsely chop, then transfer to a medium bowl and add the scallion, 1½ tablespoons olive oil, the lime juice, and a few pinches of salt.

Place the beans, a splash of olive oil, and a big pinch of salt in a separate bowl and coarsely mash with a fork until the beans are just spreadable.

Brush one side of 6 tortillas with olive oil, then arrange them, oiled-side down, on a baking sheet. Divide the black beans over 6 of the tortillas (about 2 heaping tablespoons per tortilla). Top with a generous spoonful of the salsa, a layer of the broccoli rabe mixture (about ⅓ cup), and ¼ cup grated cheese. Cover the quesadillas with the 6 remaining tortillas. Transfer to the oven and bake for 12 to 15 minutes, until the tortillas are lightly browned and crisp. To serve, cut into quarters and serve hot, with additional salsa and sour cream.

Roasted Tomato Salsa

One 28-ounce can whole tomatoes, juice
    strained off
2 shallots, peeled and quartered
3 cloves garlic, peeled

1 jalapeño chile, seeded if desired
2 tablespoons olive oil
½ teaspoon salt
Juice of ½ lime

Preheat the oven to 425°F.

Arrange the tomatoes, shallots, garlic, and jalapeño on a rimmed baking sheet and mix with the oil. Roast for 15 to 20 minutes, until the shallot and garlic are tender and slightly blistered. Transfer to a blender, add the salt and lime juice, and blend until smooth. Taste and add more salt or lime juice as needed. Stored in an airtight container, the salsa will keep for about 5 days in the refrigerator.

A Stack of Tortillas

In this salad, tortillas act as the body of the dish—the lettuce, so to speak. They're crisped by shallow-frying, a workaround for having to use a whole pot of oil, but you can bake them as well by following the method for simple tostadas on page 58. And like the tostadas, if your tortillas are getting stale, this is a great way to make use of them. Then the tortillas are crumbled over a bright dressing and combined with ripe fruit, tomatoes, and summery herbs. It's a good dish for the patio.

Summer Tortilla Salad

SERVES 4

Vegetable or canola oil, for frying
6 corn tortillas
Salt
Juice of 2 limes (1/4 cup)
1/2 teaspoon ground cumin
1/2 teaspoon salt
Pinch sugar
1/4 red onion, sliced into strips

3 tablespoons olive oil
1 big ripe tomato, chopped,
    or 1 cup halved cherry tomatoes
1 big ripe stone fruit, such as a peach or
    nectarine, or equivalent weight in
    plums, apricots, or a mango
Kernels from 2 ears corn
Handful mint, basil, or cilantro leaves

Pour about 1/2 inch of vegetable oil into a skillet set over medium heat. When hot—test by dipping an edge of a tortilla into the oil; it should sizzle immediately—fry the tortillas one by one, flipping them once, until lightly browned and crisped, about 2 minutes per tortilla. Transfer to a paper towel—lined plate and sprinkle with salt, stacking them as you go.

Whisk together the lime juice, cumin, salt, and sugar in a medium bowl, then add the onion. Let stand for about 10 minutes, then stir in the oil. Add the tomato, stone fruit, and corn. A few minutes before you're ready to serve, break the tortillas over the salad, folding gently to combine, then, when ready to eat, stir in the herbs.

These enchiladas are filled with wilted hearty, slow-cooked Swiss chard—which makes for a surprisingly substantial meal when given the enchilada treatment. You can also use Marinated Greens (page 54) here—you'll need about 2 heaping cups. I highly recommend adding Roasted Chard Stems (page 168) in here—they bring excellent texture and their mild, funky flavor really amplifies the chard. But the filling welcomes any number of other additions, including black beans, crumbled feta, corn kernels, or sautéed summer squash. You can assemble your enchiladas up to a day in advance, and then bake before it's time to eat.

Swiss Chard Enchiladas in Red Sauce

SERVES 4

3 tablespoons olive oil, divided
2 bunches Swiss chard, stems removed
    and reserved for Roasted Chard Stems
Salt
Additional fillings: 1 cup coarsely chopped
    Roasted Chard Stems (page 168), 1 cup
    cooked black beans, or ½ cup fresh or
    frozen corn kernels
½ cup crumbled cotija or feta cheese, plus
    more for garnish

1½ cups Red Enchilada Sauce
    (recipe follows)
8 to 10 small corn tortillas
Thinly sliced red onion, for garnish
Cilantro leaves and tender stems,
    for garnish
Cubed avocado, for garnish
Sour cream or crème fraîche, for garnish

Preheat the oven to 350°F.

Warm 2 tablespoons olive oil in a large skillet over low heat, then pile in the Swiss chard, incrementally if necessary. Cook until wilted and tender, low and slow, 10 to 15 minutes, or more—you don't want too much chew left in the greens. Gather them to one side of the pan and press with a wooden spoon or spatula to extract their liquid, then carefully discard it. Coarsely chop the greens, then season with salt and the remaining 1 tablespoon olive oil. Stir in the cheese and any additional fillings if desired.

Spread ¼ cup of the enchilada sauce over the bottom of a 9 x 13-inch baking pan or equivalent baking dish. If your tortillas are dry and/or prone to tearing, wrap them in a lightly moistened towel and place them on a baking sheet in the oven for 10 to 15 minutes to soften up.

To assemble, brush one side of a tortilla with sauce, fill with about 2 tablespoons of the greens, and either roll the stuffed tortilla into a cigar or fold it over the filling, and place in the prepared dish. Repeat with the remaining tortillas, lining them up in the dish so that they fit in a snug single layer (it's fine if there's overlap). Spoon the remaining sauce over the enchiladas, spreading it over any dry patches of tortilla. Transfer to the oven and bake for 15 to 20 minutes, until the sauce has reduced a bit and is bubbling around the edges. Watch closely toward the end, as it can dry out very quickly. Serve hot, garnished with additional cheese, red onion, cilantro, avocado, and sour cream, as desired.

A Stack of Tortillas

Red Enchilada Sauce

Here's a simple tomato sauce perfect for enchiladas. Its spice comes from ancho chile powder, which has a mild but assertively smoky heat. Alternatively, you can soak two whole dried ancho chiles in hot water until soft, then trim out the stem, seeds, and ribs, and blend them into the sauce using the strained soaking liquid for the water below. But I typically find the ground chile powder to be easier to find at grocery stores than the whole dried chiles.

One 14.5-ounce can tomatoes
(whole, crushed, or diced)
3 tablespoons olive oil
2 tablespoons ancho chile powder

1 teaspoon sugar
¾ teaspoon salt
½ teaspoon dried cumin
½ teaspoon dried oregano

Combine all the ingredients in a blender along with ¾ cup water. Blend until smooth, adding up to ½ cup more water to thin the sauce. Taste for seasoning. In an airtight container, it'll keep for 3 days in the refrigerator.

Roasted Chard Stems

MAKES 1½ TO 2 CUPS

These roasted chard stems offer a great way to put potential waste to delicious end. They're silky and tender and have a flavor vaguely reminiscent of asparagus, and I love them. In addition to adding them to the Swiss Chard Enchiladas, you could use them as a garnish or as a component of a grain bowl or an omelet, or just make them as a treat. Wide, thick stems work best. Unfortunately kale and other hearty green stems are too fibrous to enjoy when cooked this way.

Stems from 1 or 2 bunches Swiss chard
Olive oil

Salt
Freshly ground black pepper

Preheat the oven to 400°F.

Trim any browned or frayed parts from the cut ends of the chard stems. Arrange them in a single layer on a baking sheet. Drizzle liberally with olive oil, sprinkle with salt and black pepper, then toss to coat evenly. Transfer to the oven and roast for 15 to 20 minutes, until blistered a bit and tender when a knife is inserted into the thickest parts. Eat warm or at room temperature.

Here's a very simple soup made from pantry ingredients that's easily elevated with a spicy jalapeño relish and freshly baked tortilla chips. Stale tortillas make good candidates, or feel free to use store-bought tortilla chips rather than baking off your own. But be sure to experiment with the toppings—they are what make soups like this fun.

Tortilla Soup with Charred Jalapeño Relish

SERVES 4

5 tablespoons olive oil, divided
1 medium onion, sliced
3 cloves garlic, sliced
1 teaspoon ground cumin
1 teaspoon chili powder
Salt
½ teaspoon dried oregano
One 28-ounce can diced or
    crushed tomatoes
4 cups water or light vegetable broth
1 tablespoon butter (optional)

3 jalapeño chiles
¼ small red onion, minced
Juice of 1 lime
4 corn or flour tortillas, cut into strips
    (see headnote)
Topping ideas: poached eggs, cubed
    avocado, shaved radishes, quick-pickled
    onions or cucumbers, cotija
    or feta cheese, shredded jack or cheddar
    cheese, sour cream

Warm 3 tablespoons of the oil in a large saucepan or Dutch oven over medium heat, then add the onion, garlic, cumin, chili powder, 1 teaspoon salt, and the oregano. Cook for 6 to 8 minutes, stirring periodically, until the onion is softened. Add the tomatoes and water or broth. Bring to a simmer and cook for 15 minutes. Stir in the butter for a little extra richness, if desired.

Preheat the oven to 350°F.

Meanwhile, set the jalapeños directly over the high flame of a gas burner. Cook, turning them over in the flame using metal tongs, until the skins are blackened all over, 4 to 6 minutes. (If you don't have a gas burner, blister the jalapeños under the broiler, set on high heat, rotating them periodically until blackened all over.) Place in a small bowl and cover with plastic wrap to allow them to steam for 10 minutes. Rub off the skins (you may want to use gloved hands), then trim out and discard the seeds and ribs. Coarsely chop the flesh, place in a bowl, and add the red onion, lime juice, a pinch of salt, and 1 tablespoon of the remaining olive oil.

Pile the tortilla strips on a baking sheet and toss with the remaining 1 tablespoon olive oil and a pinch of salt. Spread into an even layer and bake for 8 to 12 minutes, until crisp.

Ladle the soup into bowls and add a spoonful of the jalapeño relish. Top with a good handful of the tortilla strips, plus toppings as desired, and serve.

CHAPTER 12

A Head of Cabbage

Poor cabbage, an unsung hero of vegetables if there ever was one. Unlike juicy summer tomatoes, or a striped and stately winter squash, or a perfectly buttery and blemish-free avocado, cabbage doesn't get many people excited. It's not sexy. Perhaps it's because of its cruciferous odor when cooked, or that as a cold-weather crop it's one of the last veg standing at the end of an endless winter, or because we primarily think of it only as the lead ingredient in a mayo-laden picnic side dish. It's become kind of a consolation prize when there aren't any other vegetables to eat—the kitchen friend that's so dependably *there* for you that beyond taking it for granted, it can be hard not to get a little contemptuous of it. Cabbage? *You?* Ugh, fine.

Let's put an end to that disparagement now. Besides being cheap and plentifully available, cabbage is a nutrient powerhouse—rich in vitamins K and C, as well as the amino acid glutamine and dozens of other vitamins and minerals. Cabbage is also an impressively versatile vegetable. Stiff leaves wrapped so tightly around their core that they seem suctioned in place will melt to a fraction of their former selves and become deeply sweet when left on the heat. In raw treatments like slaw, its bright notes are offset by a cool, quenching texture—the flavor of good water, which I mean as a compliment. It's famously fermentable, used as the basis for popular condiments like sauerkraut and kimchi. And if you've ever been unwittingly in possession of a head of cabbage, you've probably discovered its astounding yield: one heavy head can easily last a week.

At the market, choose cabbages that, well, look right: that don't have deep blemishes or frayed outer leaves, appear to have tight heads through to the core, and that feel heavy. Green and red cabbages have thicker, sturdier leaves, whereas those of Napa and Savoy cabbages are more delicate, which informs how you should set out to cook with them. In raw treatments, the sturdy ones most often benefit from salting, where the sliced vegetable is tossed in salt and left to drain for a bit; this softens its texture and helps to season the vegetable. Softer cabbages don't always need this. And in roasted and other cooked preparations, the sturdy green and red cabbages often need a greater amount of cooking time to soften than their more delicate counterparts.

If you're someone who is cabbage averse, I recommend starting with the soups in this chapter. In soup, cabbage really shines, becoming sweet and earthy, comforting and warming. The white bean and cabbage soup on page 181, enriched with nutty Gruyère cheese, is a revelation—in my kitchen I refer to it as a dish for cabbage haters, because it's the kind of thing that opens eyes. What makes that soup really work is the cheese, because when cabbage is paired with something rich—a drizzle of toasted sesame oil, or plain yogurt, or tangy feta, or fried into crispy fritters—the vegetable drops its humble pretenses completely.

Five Slaws

Coleslaw highlights one of cabbage's most winning attributes: Being a cold weather crop, it'll keep a very long time. Likewise, these salads, once packed up, will stay good for a few days, making them perfect candidates for packed lunches.

CHARRED SCALLION SLAW

SERVES 4

My well-established love for charred scallions finds a home in this slaw, where their deep savoriness is a perfect foil to snappy, refreshing, sweet Napa cabbage. Milder rice vinegar would make a nice alternative to the white wine vinegar, but the combination of almonds and either basil or mint is an essential finish to the salad, lending it crunch and a distinctive aromatic finish.

½ medium head Napa cabbage, sliced about ⅛ inch thick (about 6 cups)

Salt

Pinch sugar

2 tablespoons white wine or champagne vinegar

1 bunch scallions, ends trimmed

Olive oil

2 tablespoons fresh lemon juice

½ teaspoon honey

Freshly ground black pepper

¼ cup packed basil or mint leaves, coarsely chopped

¼ cup toasted almonds, coarsely chopped

In a large bowl, toss the cabbage with ½ teaspoon salt and the sugar. Let stand for 20 minutes (as you prepare the rest of the ingredients), then toss with 1 tablespoon of the vinegar.

Cut the scallions in half lengthwise, so that they all fit in a skillet. Heat a medium skillet over medium-high heat. Add a splash of oil, then the scallions and a pinch of salt, spreading the scallions out in as best a single layer as you can manage. Sear them on both sides until charred and the white parts are tender, 6 to 8 minutes; you'll want to press down on them periodically using a spatula to encourage them to char. Transfer to a cutting board and, when cool enough to handle, chop to a coarse mush.

Combine the scallions and the remaining 1 tablespoon vinegar, ¼ teaspoon salt, 3 tablespoons olive oil, the lemon juice, honey, and several grinds of black pepper in a small bowl. Stir with a fork to combine and taste, adding more salt or oil as necessary. Stir in the basil.

To serve, toss the cabbage with most of the dressing, adding additional dressing as needed. Just before serving, sprinkle with the chopped almonds.

KALE-CABBAGE SLAW WITH QUINOA AND BROWN SUGAR–DIJON VINAIGRETTE

SERVES 4 TO 6 AS A SIDE

Here's a substantial slaw, where kale—a botanical cousin of cabbage—is finely chopped and salted along with the green cabbage, lending a vibrant chlorophyll green to the finished salad. The addition of cooked quinoa, as an accent to the vegetables rather than enough to turn this into a grain salad, makes this a nutritious lunchtime affair. It packs very well for lunches and car trips. And the sweet-tangy brown sugar–Dijon vinaigrette can and should absolutely be utilized in other grain salads.

½ cup quinoa

1 small head green cabbage (about 1½ pounds), quartered and cored

1 bunch Tuscan or curly kale, frayed ends trimmed, roughly chopped (stems and all)

2 teaspoons salt, divided

1 teaspoon sugar

3 tablespoons olive oil

1½ tablespoons apple cider vinegar

2 teaspoons whole-grain mustard

2 tablespoons brown sugar

3 dashes angostura bitters (optional)

2 tablespoons sliced toasted almonds, or chopped toasted walnuts

Combine the quinoa and 1 cup water in a small saucepan. Bring to a boil, then reduce to a bare simmer, cover, and cook for 15 minutes, or until the grains are tender and the curly germ of the seed is exposed. If there's unabsorbed water in the pan, drain it off. Fluff with a fork and allow to cool.

Meanwhile, cut each wedge of cabbage into 3 or 4 pieces, so that they're small enough to fit through the feed tube of a food processor. In a food processor fitted with the slicing blade, slice the cabbage into thin shavings. (You can also cut the cabbage by hand or with a mandoline.) Transfer to a large bowl.

Now fit the food processor with the chopping blade, then add the kale, in batches if necessary. Pulse to finely chop the kale, then add to the bowl with the cabbage. Sprinkle with 1½ teaspoons salt and the sugar and use your hands to gently "massage" the vegetables. Let stand for about 15 minutes to soften and release some liquid. Discard the liquid.

In a small jar, combine the olive oil, vinegar, mustard, brown sugar, bitters, if using, and remaining ½ teaspoon salt and shake until emulsified. Stir the quinoa into the cabbage-kale mixture, then add the dressing to taste. Sprinkle the slaw with the nuts just before serving.

SOUR CREAM SLAW WITH FENNEL

SERVES 4 TO 6

If you're tired of mayonnaise-based coleslaw, this sour cream version may generate more interest. Its creamy tang marries beautifully with the mild licorice flavor of fennel, which is amplified by herbes de Provence, a French blend of dried herbs that often includes thyme, oregano, rosemary, savory, and sometimes lavender.

1 small Savoy or Napa cabbage, finely shredded (about 6 cups)

1 medium fennel bulb, cored and very thinly sliced, fronds reserved

¼ cup sour cream

1 tablespoon olive oil

1 tablespoon fresh lemon juice

1 teaspoon herbes de Provence

½ teaspoon salt, or to taste

¼ teaspoon sugar

Pinch red pepper flakes

In a serving bowl, combine the cabbage and fennel.

In a small bowl, stir together the sour cream, olive oil, lemon juice, herbes de Provence, sugar, and red pepper flakes. Taste and season with salt. Add most of the dressing to the cabbage and fennel and taste, adding more if needed (you may have some dressing left over). Coarsely chop about 3 tablespoons of the fennel fronds and stir them in. You can eat this slaw immediately, but the flavors will meld a bit after an hour or so at room temperature.

HONEY-SOY SLAW WITH TOFU AND SESAME SEEDS

SERVES 4 TO 6

In this main-course coleslaw, you can use a store-bought baked tofu—one that's smoked or marinated with soy sauce–based flavorings works well—or if you happen to have them on hand, the Honey-Orange Tofu (page 36), Balsamic–Soy Sauce Tofu (page 42), or Pineapple-Sriracha Tofu (page 41) are all good options. And if you wish to embrace the throwback vibe of an "Oriental Chicken Salad" (a dish my family ate often growing up despite its problematic name), crunch up half of a package of Top Ramen noodles into the salad just before serving.

6 cups shredded Napa or green cabbage

Salt, if needed

1 orange

2 tablespoons olive oil

2 tablespoons rice vinegar or apple cider vinegar

4 teaspoons soy sauce

1 tablespoon honey

Freshly ground black pepper

One 6-ounce block baked tofu or ½ recipe homemade baked tofu (see headnote), cubed or sliced into matchsticks

4 radishes, thinly sliced

4 scallions, green and white parts, thinly sliced

3 tablespoons toasted sesame seeds

If using green cabbage, toss with ½ teaspoon salt in a colander and let stand for about 20 minutes to drain.

Prepare the orange: Trim off the top and bottom ends, then cut off all the peel and pith. Holding the peeled fruit in your hand over a large bowl to collect the juices, trim the fruit free of its membranes, letting the citrus supremes fall into the bowl with the juice. Break up the segments into halves or thirds.

SOUR CREAM SLAW
WITH FENNEL,
PAGE 174

KALE-CABBAGE SLAW WITH QUINOA AND
BROWN SUGAR–DIJON VINAIGRETTE,
PAGE 173

HONEY-SOY SLAW WITH
TOFU AND SESAME SEEDS,
PAGE 175

CHARRED SCALLION SLAW,
PAGE 173

RED SLAW WITH APPLES,
CURRANTS, AND YOGURT,
PAGE 178

In a small jar, combine the olive oil, vinegar, soy sauce, honey, and several grinds of black pepper. Seal it and shake vigorously to combine.

Add the cabbage, tofu, radishes, and scallions to the bowl with the orange. Toss with most of the dressing and taste, adding more if needed (you may have some dressing left over). Stir in the sesame seeds just before serving.

RED SLAW WITH APPLES, CURRANTS, AND YOGURT

SERVES 4 TO 6

This is a bright slaw for cool weather, with color in the form of red cabbage (which turns pink as you fold in the yogurt-based dressing) and crunch in the form of crisp apple. Then there are the currants—the step of soaking them softens and reconstitutes them to something of their former ripe-fruit glory, but also saturates them with the tang of red wine vinegar so that they become little bursts of flavor.

6 cups thinly sliced red cabbage

Salt

¼ cup currants

3 tablespoons red wine vinegar

1 tart apple

¼ cup plain full-fat yogurt

1 tablespoon olive oil

1 tablespoon fresh lemon juice

½ teaspoon honey

Freshly ground black pepper

3 tablespoons chopped dill

Combine the cabbage with ½ teaspoon salt in a colander and let drain and soften for 15 to 20 minutes.

In a small saucepan, combine the currants and vinegar. Bring to a simmer, then remove from the heat, allowing the currants to soak up the remaining liquid.

Hold the apple stem-side up, then slice off the flesh in four cuts close to the core. Lay each piece flat on the cutting board and slice into thin wedges.

In a large bowl, whisk together the yogurt, oil, lemon juice, honey, ½ teaspoon salt, and several grinds of black pepper. Add the drained cabbage, apples, currants, and dill, fold to combine, and serve.

SLAW

A hearty slaw can be a meal in itself, and keeps so well that it seems as if it could have been designed specially for packed lunches and make-ahead cooking. But beyond exploring the many possibilities and different directions for coleslaw, it also has a range of applications. As a way to help think of slaw as a condiment or component of a meal, here are a few ideas and recommendations.

AS A SIDE: Slaw is always a great addition to a spread—it's classic with barbecue, alongside seasonal salads, ripe fruit, grilled vegetables and tofu, and equally at home among holiday food, offering something fresh and crunchy to contrast all the richness. And for weeknight meals, I serve slaw in place of a green salad, usually with dishes like roasted vegetables or tofu, baked or braised beans, or fried rice or grain salads.

ON A SANDWICH, A WRAP, OR TACO: In a sandwich or wrap, all you need is a boiled (or steamed; see page 111) egg or a few pieces of firm tofu to accompany it. It is also a distinctive topping for veggie burgers. Slaw makes a very straightforward taco filling (following any of the methods for warming tortillas on page 153), with or without some beans in there.

IN A GRAIN BOWL: Treat the slaw as a topping for a grain bowl, using a little extra dressing to season the grains. Round it out with some complementary herbs or salad greens, and for protein, a poached or boiled egg, cooked beans, or cubes of tofu.

This fantastic soup is inspired by a Martha Rose Shulman recipe, from her *New York Times* "Recipes for Health" column, where cabbage is cooked in a combination of broth and milk. My adaptation tastes sophisticated even without any dairy (thanks to cabbage, that chameleon, showing off a whole new side of itself when cooked), but the Gruyère makes the soup absolutely elegant. I've added white beans for heft and creaminess. Taste carefully for seasoning toward the end—I find that after adding the cheese I need to add a bit more salt to bring the flavors into balance.

Cheesy Cabbage and White Bean Soup

SERVES 4 TO 6

2 tablespoons olive oil

1 medium onion, or 2 leeks, white parts only, chopped

2 cloves garlic, minced

½ medium head green or Savoy cabbage, shredded (about 5 cups)

½ teaspoon salt, plus more as needed

Two 15-ounce cans cannellini beans, including the liquid, or 4 cups cooked white beans with a few ladlesful of their broth

5 cups vegetable broth, or 1 tablespoon bouillon base dissolved in 5 cups water

1 cup shredded Gruyère or Parmesan cheese, or 1½ cups shredded sharp cheddar

Freshly ground black pepper

Fried breadcrumbs or croutons, for serving (optional; see page 182)

Warm the olive oil in a soup pot over medium heat, then stir in the onions and garlic, followed by the cabbage and salt. Cook for about 5 minutes, until just starting to soften, then add the beans and broth. Bring to a simmer, then cover and cook for 30 minutes, or until the vegetables are tender and the broth is flavorful. Remove from the heat and add the cheese a handful at a time, stirring until it melts into the broth. Taste and season with additional salt, as needed (depending on the saltiness of your vegetable stock or bouillon, it may need quite a bit of salt, as the beans really soak it up), and a few grinds of pepper. Serve hot, topped with breadcrumbs or croutons, if desired.

BREAD AS A
GARNISH

Bread can add body and contrast to soups, salads, and baked gratin-like dishes—oftentimes it's just the thing to fix a dish that's missing a crunchy-salty element. If you've got a loaf of bread kicking around in your kitchen and it's starting to get stale, just put it in your freezer rather than throwing it away—you can turn it into breadcrumbs later on. And even the most dried-out end of bread can be pounded up in a mortar and pestle. Then, following one of the methods below, once you've got breadcrumbs, store them in an airtight container in your cupboard, freezer, or refrigerator for easy access to use as a garnish.

BAKED CROUTONS: Cut or tear bread into roughly uniform sizes, then toss with a few glugs of olive oil and salt and black pepper to taste. You can also add a pinch of dried herbs (herbes de Provence, thyme, sage, or any flavors that will complement what's in your dish). Spread out on a baking sheet and bake in a 325°F oven, stirring every 10 minutes or so, until crisp and dried out (be thorough: If the bread is still chewy in the center, the croutons will become rock-hard once they cool). Once cooled, store in an airtight container.

TOASTED BREADCRUMBS: If you start with semi-fresh bread, tear it into small pieces and pulse in a food processor until coarsely ground. Spread out on a baking sheet and toast at 300°F, stirring often, until completely dried out, or just set the sheet in the oven and leave it there overnight to dry. The drier the bread is, the less time it'll need to spend in the oven. Or if you have a few pieces of completely stale (aka, already dried) bread lying around, you can pound it into crumbs in a mortar and pestle. In either case, store the crumbs in an airtight container. To revive these dried crumbs and use them as, say, a garnish for soup, cook them in a skillet with a bit of oil and a pinch of salt until golden.

FRESH FRIED CROUTONS: This method is for fresh bread, when you've got a chewy loaf of sourdough or other bread with some pliability. Trim off the crusts and tear it into craggy pieces. Warm a thin layer of olive oil in a skillet over medium heat, then add the bread—don't crowd the pan—and cook, tossing every now and then, until golden brown and crisp on the outside but still chewy on the inside. Drain on paper towels and sprinkle with salt. Cook these to order—because the bread is still soft and fresh inside, they'll go stale as they sit—and serve with soups or salads.

One time when I served this dish at a dinner party, a guest, when prodded for feedback, said that it tasted like "what I always want roasted cabbage to taste like." Bull's-eye, I thought. It's tender and sweet, with the maple and vinegar doing the work of making roasted cabbage taste most like itself. Save leftovers to repurpose in other meals: Use it in bowls (it is excellent topped with a fried or poached egg), in sandwiches, or as a filling for tacos.

Perfect Roasted Cabbage

SERVES 4 TO 6

1 head green cabbage, sliced through
   the core into 12 wedges
3 tablespoons olive oil
Salt

Freshly ground black pepper
2 tablespoons red or white wine vinegar
2 tablespoons maple syrup
1 tablespoon butter

Preheat the oven to 425°F.

Arrange the cabbage wedges on a baking sheet. Drizzle with the olive oil and sprinkle with salt and black pepper. Roast until well colored, blistered in spots, and tender, 30 to 40 minutes, flipping once halfway through. Toward the end of cooking time, heat the vinegar and maple syrup in a small saucepan until simmering, then whisk in the butter. Pour this over the hot cabbage, then return to the hot oven for 3 minutes more. Serve hot, warm, or at room temperature.

The borscht method of using the beet cooking liquid as stock is one that I love—it's resourceful and lends the finished soup a pure beet flavor and very saturated color. Cabbage isn't always in borscht, but the crunch of Savoy cabbage is more than welcome in this cooling, refreshing, and surprisingly satiating soup. Note that it's best not to use a strained (Greek-style) yogurt here—you want a yogurt with a runnier texture that will blend easily into the soup and keep the broth on the thinner side.

Borscht with Cabbage and Golden Beets

SERVES 4 TO 6

1½ pounds golden beets
Salt
2 cups shredded Savoy cabbage
¼ small white or red onion, minced
2 teaspoons white wine vinegar
1 medium cucumber, peeled, seeded, and chopped

⅔ cup plain yogurt, plus more (optional), for garnish
½ cup chopped dill
Freshly ground black pepper
Olive oil, to finish

If the beets are large, peel and quarter them; small beets can be peeled after cooking. Place the beets in a large saucepan and cover with 5 cups water. Bring to a boil over high heat, then add 1½ teaspoons salt and reduce to a simmer. Cook until the beets are completely tender and easily pierced with a paring knife, 20 to 30 minutes (cut one open and taste to be sure). Use a slotted spoon to transfer the beets to a cutting board and let them cool until safe to handle. If unpeeled, peel the beets using a few paper towels, then chop them into bite-size pieces. Reserve the cooking liquid.

Meanwhile, place the cabbage and onion in a large heat-safe bowl and toss with the remaining ½ teaspoon salt and the vinegar. While the beet cooking liquid is still hot, strain it to remove any debris, then measure 3½ cups and pour it over the cabbage. Stir in the chopped beets. Cool completely, then refrigerate until thoroughly chilled.

Stir in the cucumber, yogurt, and dill. Season with salt and black pepper. Make sure to serve this soup cold, and ideally the next day after the flavors have had time to meld. Drizzle with olive oil and garnish with dollops of yogurt, if desired.

This main-dish salad is full of texture, with tender beans, crunchy cabbage, creamy feta, and little wisps of fried onions. It's a longtime favorite recipe of mine, one that came about, as so many recipes do, from having a few odds and ends lying around—in this case, it was onion-frying oil, a little tub of cooked lentils, and half a head of Napa cabbage. The flavorful oil left over from making frizzled onions is essential to the vinaigrette, giving the salad a savory depth—so make sure not to discard it. While the fried onions won't stay crisp for long, the way that they soften in the salad as leftovers sit is still very tasty.

Lentil, Cabbage, and Feta Salad with Frizzled Onions

SERVES 4 TO 6

½ cup brown, black, or dark green lentils
Salt
½ medium white or yellow onion
Olive oil
5 cups sliced Napa, green, or Savoy
   cabbage
¼ teaspoon sugar

2 tablespoons red or white wine vinegar
2 teaspoons Dijon mustard
¼ teaspoon honey
½ cup crumbled feta cheese
½ cup coarsely chopped toasted almonds
½ cup dill fronds or whole parsley leaves

Combine the lentils with 1 cup water and ½ teaspoon salt in a small saucepan. Bring to a simmer, cover, and cook until tender, 12 to 18 minutes, depending on which lentils you use. Drain off any liquid left in the pan and allow to cool.

Meanwhile, slice the onion into paper-thin wisps, preferably using a mandoline, or working carefully with a chef's knife. Warm about ¼ inch of olive oil in a small skillet over medium heat. Dip a piece of onion into it to ensure it's properly hot—it should sizzle immediately—then add all the onions. Cook, stirring often with a fork, until they get crisp and turn a reddish-brown color, 10 to 20 minutes. Watch carefully for the final few minutes, as they burn easily. Use a slotted spoon to transfer them to a paper towel–lined plate and sprinkle with salt. Save the oil!

When the oil has cooled until it's safe to handle, strain it through a fine-mesh sieve or coffee filter to remove all solids into a glass jar (I use a 3-inch strainer for this task).

Toss the cabbage, ½ teaspoon salt, and the sugar in a colander and let soften for 15 to 30 minutes, then gently press with a spatula to drain off any excess liquid.

Combine the vinegar, mustard, and honey in a jar, along with 3 tablespoons of the cooled onion-cooking oil. Shake to emulsify.

Fold together the cabbage, lentils, cheese, almonds, and dill fronds or parsley leaves with most of the dressing in a serving bowl. Taste and add more dressing if needed (you may have some dressing left over). Pile the frizzled onions on top, tossing them into the salad at the table as it's being served.

A Head of Cabbage

This is a bit of a "cabbage two ways" kind of dish, where the long-fermented cabbage flavors a quick sauté of fresh cabbages. Together, they demonstrate the versatility of the vegetable. Serve this as a side dish, as a component in grain bowls, over steamed rice with a fried egg, or as a quesadilla filling using flour tortillas and sharp cheddar cheese. The kimchi brine is the liquid that collects in the jar—see page 117 for instructions on how to extract it.

Cabbage and Kimchi Sauté

SERVES 4

1 tablespoon olive oil
5 cups cubed cabbage, any variety
½ teaspoon salt
Pinch sugar

½ cup packed cabbage kimchi, drained
  and chopped
1 teaspoon soy sauce
1 teaspoon kimchi brine (see page 117)
Freshly ground black pepper

Heat a medium skillet over medium-high heat and add the olive oil. Pile in the cabbage and add the salt and sugar. Cook, tossing every now and then, just until beginning to soften, 5 to 10 minutes, depending on the cabbage variety. Clear a little space in the center of the pan and add the kimchi, allowing it to sizzle for a few seconds before stirring it in. Cook for a few minutes, raising the heat if necessary so as to encourage some searing. Once the cabbage is tender, clear another space in the middle of the pan and pour in the soy sauce and kimchi brine, allowing it to bubble before stirring it into the cabbage until the pan is dry. Add a few grinds of black pepper, then serve hot, warm, or at room temperature.

These fritters are a go-to when I've got vegetable odds and ends lying around, because pretty much anything tastes great when fried up in fritter form! I make them with raw shredded cabbage, while also cleaning out my leftovers by throwing in some Roasted Cauliflower or Broccoli (page 192) or a handful of chopped Roasted Mushrooms (page 136). Bagged shredded cabbage or "broccoli slaw" works great, too. Opt for sturdy vegetables, and know that anything inedible or not tasty raw must be cooked before getting mixed into the batter. Add a few tablespoons of chopped kimchi to take the flavor profile in a vaguely Korean-pancake direction.

Cabbage (or Other Vegetable) Fritters

MAKES 10 TO 12 FRITTERS

¾ cup plus 2 tablespoons all-purpose
    flour or chickpea flour
2 tablespoons cornstarch
1 teaspoon baking powder
½ teaspoon salt
Freshly ground black pepper
1 cup dairy milk or unflavored,
    unsweetened nondairy milk

1 egg
2 cups shredded cabbage
1 cup coarsely chopped vegetables
    (see headnote) or additional cabbage
2 scallions, green and white parts,
    thinly sliced
Olive oil, for cooking the fritters

Whisk together the flour, cornstarch, baking powder, salt, and several grinds of black pepper in a large bowl. In a separate bowl, whisk together the milk and egg, then add to the dry ingredients and stir just until smooth. Add the cabbage, chopped vegetables, and scallions.

Place a skillet or griddle over medium-high heat and add a thin layer of oil. Carefully drop heaping tablespoons of the batter—scooping from the bottom of the bowl so you get a balance of batter and veg in your fritter—and add to the pan, flattening it out a bit with the back of the spoon. Don't overcrowd. Cook until golden brown and crisp on the bottom, 2 to 3 minutes, then carefully flip and repeat on the other side. Sprinkle with a bit of salt and serve hot.

CHAPTER 13

Crowns of Cauliflower or Broccoli

Cauliflower and broccoli have many similarities: they're both highly nutritious cruciferous vegetables, can be polarizing among adults and children alike, and share plenty of cross-over in cooking methods. Sometimes I combine them in the same dish or on the same baking sheet, as their similar shape and texture means they've got similar cooking times, and I certainly take liberties swapping one for the other in recipes. And when I'm at the grocery store, I tend to go for one *or* the other, alternating my choice from week to week.

I like these vegetables for many of the reasons that they're currently in vogue. They deliver a high dose of nutrients in a low dose of calories and tend to be quite filling. Plant-focused cooks have found countless ways to creatively manipulate cauliflower and broccoli to function as sneaky stand-ins for other foods—such as blitzing cauliflower in a food processor to make a healthier "rice" for stir-fries and bowls; searing thick cross-sections of cauliflower or making lengthwise quarters of broccoli through the stalk to make "steaks" that can assume center-of-the-plate status; and whizzing up cauliflower with soaked cashews and nutritional yeast to mimic creamy cheese in baked dishes.

I most often opt for simple treatments, breaking heads into florets and roasting them in olive oil with salt and black pepper. Roasting is the best way to cook them, in my opinion, because it accentuates their sweet nuttiness and minimizes their sulfurous odor. While you probably already know how to roast broccoli and cauliflower, I start this chapter with a basic roasting recipe, one meant to serve as a jumping-off point for salads and sandwiches and other dishes later on.

One important difference between the two is their stalks: Broccoli ideally has a long stalk attached. Some recipes instruct you to discard this, but I think it's the most delicious part. It's encased in a fibrous skin, which needs to be peeled off using a vegetable peeler or a paring knife. Once the pale inner flesh of the stalk is exposed, slice it into thick slabs on the bias and add it to the pan with the rest of the broccoli for roasting. As for cauliflower, cooks are often instructed to trim out and discard the core, but similar to broccoli, this part of the vegetable is delicious, too. It's a bit denser than the florets; cut it into smaller pieces so it cooks at a similar rate to the florets.

I love all the colorful cauliflower options—dusty purples and oranges, deep yellows and pale greens, and then there's romanesco, with its kaleidoscopic pattern that makes it look as if it's straight out of a Pixar film. These different varieties have subtle differences—most of the colored ones take longer to mature, and they're denser vegetables than standard white cauliflower—but for the purposes of this book they're interchangeable in these recipes.

An extra sheet of roasted cauliflower or broccoli will set you on the right foot for numerous future meals. Don't hesitate to use pre-cut or bagged broccoli or cauliflower, as it works perfectly in this treatment (even if it's more expensive, pound for pound, as you're paying for the labor). If you prefer steamed or boiled broccoli, you can substitute it in the following recipes that call for roasted cauliflower. And while you may have your own way of roasting cauliflower or broccoli, one technique that I think makes a difference is going to the trouble of making flat surfaces. These parts of the cut vegetables caramelize more deeply than the uneven florets or other curving parts of the stem, meaning more flavor.

Roasted Cauliflower or Broccoli

MAKES ABOUT 4 CUPS

2 medium heads cauliflower or broccoli,
    outer leaves discarded
Olive oil

Salt
Freshly ground black pepper

Preheat the oven to 400°F.

Working close to the stem, cut or snap off large bunches of florets of cauliflower or broccoli. Depending on their size, halve or quarter them so that you've got a flat surface or two. For the cauliflower, cut the white core into pieces a bit smaller than the florets. For the broccoli, use a vegetable peeler or paring knife to remove the thick, fibrous skin around the stem, then cut the peeled stem into pieces the same thickness as the florets.

Divide the vegetables between two baking sheets, then drizzle generously with olive oil and sprinkle with salt and black pepper. Toss to evenly coat, then transfer to the oven and roast until tender and caramelized in parts, 20 to 30 minutes, stirring and rotating the pans once halfway through.

These make a great grab-and-go breakfast, and I love the craggy torn pieces of olive that stud them. They lend themselves to any number of variations—add scallions and feta cheese, or diced roasted peppers and oily black olives for starters. Use a nonstick muffin tin to ensure an easy release, or fit the muffin tin with paper liners before filling. To make them gluten free, substitute chickpea flour or an all-purpose gluten-free flour; there's so little flour that it makes no difference.

Cauliflower and Olive Frittata Cups

MAKES 10

1 tablespoon olive oil, plus more for greasing
4 cups Roasted Cauliflower (page 194)
5 eggs
2 tablespoons all-purpose flour or chickpea flour
¼ teaspoon kosher salt

Freshly ground black pepper
A few swipes lemon zest
¼ cup halved olives, such as Kalamata or Castelvetrano
½ cup chopped cilantro, dill, or parsley
Flaky salt

Preheat the oven to 350°F. Line 10 cups of a muffin tin with paper liners or brush them generously with olive oil.

Combine the cauliflower, eggs, flour, olive oil, kosher salt, a few grinds of black pepper, and lemon zest in a food processor or blender and process until the cauliflower is well minced but still retains texture—you don't want a completely smooth consistency. Stir in the olives and herbs. Divide the mixture among the prepared muffin cups and sprinkle each one with a pinch of flaky salt. Bake for 25 to 30 minutes, until puffed slightly and just set in the centers. Cool for about 10 minutes, then turn them out onto a wire rack. Enjoy warm, at room temperature, or cold. Stored in an airtight container or bag in the refrigerator, they'll keep for about 3 days.

This recipe is inspired by the excellent brunch menu sandwich at Sunday in Brooklyn, a restaurant fittingly in Brooklyn, where roasted cauliflower is stuffed between grilled toast with sauerkraut and a sambal-spiked aioli. It's spicy and well textured—and it gave me the idea for a variation involving kimchi. You'll want to start out with warm or room temperature cauliflower so that the sandwich is properly heated through when it's time to eat.

Cauliflower and Kimchi Sandwiches

MAKES 2 SANDWICHES

2 cups Roasted Cauliflower (page 192), coarsely chopped
¼ cup coarsely chopped kimchi and its juices
1 tablespoon olive oil, plus additional for grilling sandwiches
Salt

Freshly ground black pepper
4 slices multigrain sandwich bread
About 2 tablespoons mayonnaise
2 slices mild-flavored, good-melting cheese (provolone, Monterey Jack, mild cheddar)

In a medium bowl, combine the cauliflower, kimchi, and olive oil. Toss to evenly coat and season with salt and black pepper.

Warm a thin film of olive oil in a wide skillet over medium heat. Spread one side of each slice of the bread with the mayonnaise and place them, mayo-side up, in the skillet. Divide the cauliflower mixture over 2 of the slices and lay the cheese over the other 2 slices. Cook for about 3 minutes, until the bottoms are golden brown and the cheese is melted. Close up the sandwiches, slice in half, and serve hot.

Here's a tabbouleh-inspired salad, where cauliflower replaces the traditional bulgur but stays in big enough chunks that you can pierce it with a fork, and the herbs are left whole rather than finely chopped. The result is something entirely different, of course, but equally enjoyable—it's the sort of salad to heap inside a warm pita with a dollop of freshly made hummus or cold yogurt, or add to a summery picnic spread and enjoy al fresco.

Cauliflower and Herb Salad

SERVES 4 TO 6 AS A SIDE

2 cups Roasted Cauliflower (page 192)
Leaves from 1 small bunch parsley
  (about 3 cups)
½ cup loosely packed mint leaves,
  large ones torn
2 small cucumbers, chopped

1 cup halved or quartered cherry tomatoes
2 tablespoons fresh lemon juice, plus more
  as needed
2 tablespoons olive oil
½ teaspoon salt, plus more as needed
Freshly ground black pepper

Chop the cauliflower so that the largest pieces are about the size of an almond and place in a serving bowl. Add the parsley, mint, cucumbers, and tomatoes and toss to combine. Add the lemon juice, olive oil, salt, and a few grinds of black pepper. Stir, then taste and add additional salt or lemon juice as needed. For best results, add the herbs just prior to serving, before they start to wilt and discolor.

This creamy soup has a pleasant autumnal flavor profile that's anchored by maple and perfumed with apple. It requires very little active time in the kitchen, and it employs one of the greatest nondairy enrichments I've encountered: soaked cashews are blitzed into the soup to thicken and add their delicate flavor. The soup doesn't necessarily need garnishes beyond a drizzle of olive oil, but toasted sunflower or pumpkin seeds, a spoonful of tahini, some chopped wilted greens, or a handful of tender salad greens would all be nice embellishments.

Roasted Cauliflower and Apple Soup

SERVES 4

1 medium head cauliflower, leaves trimmed and broken or chopped into florets and the core chopped into small pieces
1 medium apple, cored and cut into eighths
1 medium onion, cut into eighths
3 tablespoons olive oil, plus more for drizzling

4 tablespoons maple syrup, divided
1 teaspoon salt, divided
½ cup raw cashews or skinned hazelnuts
7 cups vegetable broth, or 1 heaping tablespoon vegetable bouillon base dissolved in 7 cups water
2 bay leaves

Preheat the oven to 400°F. Line a baking sheet with parchment paper.

Spread the cauliflower, apple, and onion out on the prepared sheet. Drizzle with the olive oil and 2 tablespoons of the maple syrup and sprinkle with ½ teaspoon of the salt. Use your hands to gently coat the vegetables evenly. Transfer to the oven and roast for 30 to 40 minutes, stirring once or twice, until the cauliflower is tender and the onion is soft and a bit blistered.

Meanwhile, put the nuts in a bowl and cover them with hot tap water; let stand on the counter.

Use a rubber spatula to scrape the vegetables and any sticky juices into a soup pot. Add the stock or bouillon and water, the remaining ½ teaspoon salt, and the bay leaves and bring to a boil, then turn down the heat and simmer for 25 minutes. Drain the cashews and add them to the pot, along with the remaining 2 tablespoons maple syrup. Pluck out the bay leaves.

Blend the soup until very smooth—it's best to use a standing blender, in batches, to achieve maximum creaminess; if you opt for a hand blender, be very thorough. Return to the pot and taste for seasoning. Serve hot, drizzled with a bit of olive oil.

This is one of my favorite ways to cook cauliflower: slicing it up into thin, irregularly shaped slabs (and inevitable cauliflower debris) and piling it into a hot pan, where it cooks by a combination of steaming and caramelization—the caramelization appears on its plentiful exposed surface area. If you have capers on hand, they make a nice briny substitution for the olives.

Pan-Fried Cauliflower with Olives and Lemon

SERVES 4

1 medium head cauliflower, leaves trimmed
3 tablespoons olive oil, plus more for drizzling
3 cloves garlic, thinly sliced
Red pepper flakes

½ cup pitted and halved Castelvetrano olives (or 3 tablespoons capers, rinsed)
Lemon zest and juice
Salt
Freshly ground black pepper
½ cup whole parsley leaves

Quarter the cauliflower through the stem. Trim out and discard the core (or reserve it for another use), then lay flat-side down and slice into thin slabs. (It may be necessary to cut the halves into smaller, more manageable pieces—you're aiming for bite-size pieces.) Repeat with the remaining cauliflower quarters.

Heat 3 tablespoons olive oil in a Dutch oven or wide, deep skillet over medium-high heat and add the garlic and a big pinch of red pepper flakes. Pile in the cauliflower, spreading it into an even layer. Cook for 3 to 4 minutes without disturbing, which will encourage the bottom to caramelize and blister a bit, then use a wooden spoon or spatula to gently toss. Again, cook without disturbing so as to encourage caramelization at the bottom of the pan, another 3 to 4 minutes. Repeat this process for 15 to 20 minutes, until the cauliflower is tender (but not mushy) and caramelized.

Stir in the olives or capers. Just before serving, add several swipes of lemon zest, a squeeze of lemon juice, a drizzle of olive oil, a few grinds of black pepper, and the parsley leaves. Season carefully with salt at the very end (as the olives and capers are already salty). Serve hot, warm, or at room temperature.

Crowns of Cauliflower or Broccoli

When I made this mac and cheese for my nieces, the oldest one, Zoe—who is a Kraft loyalist—wasn't sold, but her younger sister, Ali, who was four at the time, gave it a big thumbs up. While this is a substantially healthier take on the classic comfort food, it isn't meant to sidestep the dish's hallmarks with substitutions—there is still macaroni and there is still cheese. But it does succeed in scaling back on the dairy and increasing the vegetable quota from zero to a whole head of cauliflower or broccoli. When I'm short on patience, I'll eat it "stovetop style," meaning I skip the step of transferring it to a baking dish, sprinkling with breadcrumbs, and baking it.

Cauli- or Broccoli-Mac

SERVES 6

1 medium head cauliflower or broccoli, florets and core coarsely chopped, or 3 cups riced cauliflower or broccoli
Salt
3 cups medium pasta shells (conchiglie) or other similar-size pasta shape
4 tablespoons butter
1 small onion or ½ large onion, diced
Pinch red pepper flakes

2 tablespoons all-purpose flour
2 cups milk
6 ounces grated sharp cheddar cheese (about 3 cups)
1½ ounces grated Parmesan or Gruyère cheese (about ¾ cup)
1 cup coarse fresh breadcrumbs (optional, see page 182)
2 tablespoons olive oil (optional)

Place the cauliflower or broccoli in a food processor, in batches if necessary, and pulse until finely ground. (If you're using a riced version, skip this step.)

If you plan to bake the macaroni, preheat the oven to 375°F.

Bring a pot of salted water to boil and add the shells. Cook until just tender, 8 to 10 minutes, or according to the package instructions. Drain, then rinse with cool water to prevent them from sticking together.

Melt the butter in a large, oven-safe saucepan or Dutch oven over medium heat and add the onion, ¾ teaspoon salt, and the red pepper flakes. Cook until soft and translucent, about 6 minutes, then add the cauliflower or broccoli. Cook, stirring often, until tender and somewhat reduced, another 8 to 10 minutes. Stir in the flour and cook, stirring, for 1 minute, then add the milk while stirring. Bring to a boil, reduce to a simmer, and cook for 6 to 10 minutes to thicken the mixture slightly. Add the cheeses and stir until melted. Stir in the cooked pasta and taste for seasoning. You can serve the macaroni straight from the pot.

Or to bake the macaroni, spread it in a 9 x 9-inch or equivalent baking dish. Stir together the breadcrumbs, olive oil, and a pinch of salt in a small bowl and sprinkle evenly over the macaroni. Transfer to the oven and bake for 25 to 30 minutes, until bubbling along the edges and the topping is lightly browned. Let cool for about 10 minutes before serving.

Crowns of Cauliflower or Broccoli

This soup employs a technique popularized by *New York Times* columnist and cookbook author Melissa Clark in her recipe for Seared Broccoli and Potato Soup, of searing broccoli before making the soup. This helps to retain a vibrant green color in the finished soup and also introduces smoky, caramelized flavors. The addition of a small amount of rice results in a luxe, thick puree that doesn't depend on dairy. But while the soup itself is dairy- (and gluten-) free, I've offered some cheesy crunch in the form of the optional cheddar frico, a crispy cheese cracker that's simple to make on the stovetop. Onions or shallots can be substituted for the leeks, and for a vegan topping that mimics the frico, prepare a batch of frizzled shallots (page 106).

Broccoli and Leek Soup with Cheddar Frico

SERVES ABOUT 6

3 tablespoons olive oil, plus more
    for garnish
2 pounds broccoli, trimmed into florets,
    stems peeled and cut into bite-size
    pieces
Salt
2 medium leeks, white and pale green
    parts only, chopped

3 cloves garlic, coarsely chopped
½ cup white rice
1 cup whole parsley leaves and tender
    stems
Freshly ground black pepper
Fresh lemon juice
Cheddar Frico (recipe follows)

Warm 1½ tablespoons of the olive oil in a Dutch oven or soup pot over medium-high heat. Add half the broccoli and cook until charred on the bottom and glistening and bright green on the top, about 5 minutes. (Doneness doesn't matter at this point.) Transfer to a plate or bowl, then repeat with remaining broccoli. Season the broccoli with a few pinches of salt and set aside.

Remove the pot from the heat to cool off for a minute, then return to the burner over medium-low heat. Add the remaining 1½ tablespoons olive oil, followed by the leeks, garlic, and ½ teaspoon salt and cook, stirring, for 5 to 7 minutes, until softened and reduced. Add the rice, 6 cups water, and 1½ teaspoons salt. Bring to a simmer and cook for about 15 minutes, until the rice is very tender. Add the broccoli and cook for 5 minutes more. Taste the broccoli—there should be a pleasant bit of crunch left in it; it shouldn't be mushy or fading in color.

Working in batches, add the soup to a blender with the parsley and blend until smooth, then return to the pot, season with black pepper, judicious drops of lemon juice, and additional salt to taste. Serve hot, shattering a cheddar frico on top of each serving at the very last moment.

TO MAKE IN SMALL BATCHES ON THE STOVETOP: Warm a nonstick skillet over medium heat. Using about 3 tablespoons of sharp cheddar cheese per frico, arrange piles of cheese in the skillet, spacing them well apart (they'll melt and spread—you'll likely only be able to make two at a time). Cook without disturbing until they look a bit like tuiles and are golden brown. Turn off the heat and let them cool for a minute in the pan, then use a spatula to gently transfer to a plate or cutting board to finish cooling and become crisp.

TO MAKE IN LARGER BATCHES IN THE OVEN: Preheat the oven to 375°F. Line a baking sheet with parchment paper and brush it with neutrally flavored oil. Arrange piles of shredded sharp cheddar cheese, about 3 tablespoons each, no more than 8, on the baking sheet, then transfer to the oven. Bake until they look a bit like tuiles and are golden brown. Remove from the oven and allow to cool for at least 5 minutes, then use a spatula to gently transfer to a plate or cutting board to finish cooling and become crisp.

With a tub of this in the fridge—which you can loosely think of as broccoli "pesto"—a dinner of creamy green pasta is just a pot of boiling water away. Or use it as a sandwich spread, as a flavorful sauce for rice and other grain bowls, or as a dip for crackers or crudités. And if you've got an assortment of herbs, it welcomes a medley: Add mint and parsley or a few tablespoons of chopped tarragon or oregano—enough to make 1 cup packed of herbs.

Roasted Broccoli Sauce

MAKES ABOUT 1½ CUPS

¼ cup toasted almonds or walnuts
1 clove garlic, peeled
Salt
2 cups Roasted Broccoli (page 192)
1 cup packed basil leaves

3 tablespoons olive oil
¼ cup grated Parmesan cheese (optional)
Fresh lemon juice
Freshly ground black pepper

Place the nuts, garlic, and a pinch of salt in the bowl of a food processor and pulse until finely ground, scraping down the sides of the bowl as often as needed. Add the broccoli and basil and continue pulsing until everything is uniformly ground. Then with the motor running, pour in the olive oil. To lighten the consistency, add a few splashes of water with the motor running. Stir in the cheese, if using, then add a squeeze of lemon and a few grinds of black pepper. Taste and add more lemon juice or salt as needed. Stored in an airtight container in the refrigerator, this sauce will keep for 2 to 3 days.

It wasn't until I was a teenager that my family discovered the pleasure of roasted broccoli, with its succulent texture and deep, caramelized flavor. Prior to that, we ate it plainly steamed. In my adulthood I've enjoyed returning to steamed broccoli, appreciating how it cooks quickly, doesn't require preheating an oven, and tastes purely of, well, vegetables. It also takes well to almost any kind of sauce or dressing you've got. Below, I offer a few suggestions.

Steamed Broccoli and Sauces

SERVES 4 AS A SIDE

1 medium head broccoli, preferably including the stem

Separate the broccoli florets by trimming down close to the stem, so that each floret has a long stem itself. When you're left with just the base stem, use a vegetable peeler or paring knife to trim off the thick, fibrous outer skin. Then cut the peeled stem into thick coins.

Fit a saucepan with a steamer insert and fill the pan with about an inch of water. (If you don't have a steamer insert, you can omit it.) Bring to a boil, then add the broccoli, cover the pan, and cook until just tender, 4 to 7 minutes—better to have a little crunch and retain the vibrant green than to have mushy, soft broccoli. Transfer to a plate or bowl to cool. (If you cooked without the steamer insert, thoroughly drain the broccoli first.)

Dress the warm broccoli to taste or offer sauces for dipping, and serve warm or at room temperature. In addition to the suggestions below, the olive-yogurt dressing (page 70) and maple-lemon dressing (page 67) also make excellent companions for steamed broccoli.

Mustard-Turmeric Sauce

MAKES ABOUT ½ CUP

2 tablespoons whole-grain mustard
2 tablespoons white wine vinegar
1 teaspoon ground turmeric
1 teaspoon honey

¼ teaspoon salt
¼ cup olive oil
Freshly ground black pepper

Whisk together the mustard, vinegar, turmeric, honey, and salt in a small bowl. While whisking, pour in the olive oil. Season with black pepper.

Crumbled Blue Cheese Sauce

MAKES ABOUT ⅓ CUP

1 shallot, or ¼ small red onion,
    finely minced
2 tablespoons white wine vinegar
¼ teaspoon salt

¼ cup crumbled blue cheese
¼ cup olive oil
Freshly ground black pepper

Combine the shallot, vinegar, and salt in a small bowl and let stand for 5 minutes. Stir in the cheese and olive oil. Season with black pepper.

Lemon-Parmesan Sauce

MAKES ABOUT ½ CUP

1 small clove garlic, peeled
Salt
Juice of 1 lemon

¼ cup olive oil
½ cup finely grated Parmesan cheese
Freshly ground black pepper

Smash the garlic clove on a cutting board. Sprinkle it with a pinch of salt, then mince and mash using the flat side of a knife to achieve a paste. Combine the minced garlic with the lemon juice in a small bowl. Whisk in the olive oil, then stir in the cheese and plenty of black pepper.

Crowns of Cauliflower or Broccoli

CHAPTER 14

Several Summer Squash

Summer squash—that category of vegetables that includes zucchini, yellow squash, crookneck squash, pattypan, and many others (delicata and acorn squash actually belong to this same family, but with their orange flesh, longer cooking times, and flavor more fitting of the winter months, I left them in the Winter Squash chapter)—really only seem to come up in conversation, well, in the summer, when they're in abundance at the farmers market. Or at least it seems like that's the only time anyone is interested in cooking them. I, too, love summer squash in the summer, but I'm always amazed by how reliably present they are at supermarkets all year long.

I've started incorporating summer squash into my meals throughout the seasons, adding a few to my cart every week in order to play around with them in soups, curries, and baked goods. No, they don't have a ton of flavor, and yes, it's easy to cook them to mush. But they really are a cheap and nutritious vegetable. They're an excellent source of copper and manganese, and they are rich in carotenoids, which function in the body as an antioxidant. And when they are cooked properly, good things can happen.

Because of its high water content and mild flavor, tossing cut up or grated summer squash in some salt can be an essential step for a flavorful, not-waterlogged, finished dish. The process is simple: Combine your prepped (grated, sliced, or cubed) squash with salt—for every medium one, you'll need about ½ teaspoon salt—in a colander. Let stand for 15 to 20 minutes, during which time you'll watch the vegetables begin to glisten. Then you can either squeeze or blot the squash dry—it will release an alarming amount of liquid—and you're ready to proceed with the recipe.

I like how these vegetables pair so beautifully with Italian and Mediterranean flavors (tomatoes and basil), as well as Middle Eastern ones (tahini and chickpeas), and even South Asian ones (coconut milk and chiles). Their mildness means they are a foil for bold treatments. And I happen to love their mild flavor—they taste quenchingly fresh and green, with a hint of soft herbs and a note of something a little funky, like asparagus.

These recipes cover a wide range of options for incorporating summer squash into your regular cooking, from baked zucchini with honeyed marinara and goat cheese, to a cashew-based creamy soup that can be served hot or cold, to a new direction for zucchini bread (in which it finds a new home as beer bread). My hope is that you'll start adding these vegetables to your shopping basket on the regular, too.

Adding zucchini to stuffed mushrooms creates a deliciously moist filling, here accented with chopped nuts and a few other aromatics. For a vegan option, nutritional yeast, that perfect popcorn seasoning and cheese-esque lifesaver for those who abstain from dairy, works perfectly in place of the Parmesan.

Zucchini-Stuffed Mushrooms

SERVES 4 TO 6 AS AN APPETIZER

1 small zucchini (6 ounces)
Salt
Olive oil
1 small shallot, or ¼ small onion, minced
¼ cup walnuts or almonds, finely chopped
½ teaspoon lemon zest

Freshly ground black pepper
12 ounces button or cremini mushrooms
5 tablespoons panko or other coarse
    breadcrumbs, divided
2 tablespoons finely grated Parmesan
    cheese, or 2 teaspoons nutritional yeast

Preheat the oven to 400°F.

Grate the squash using the large holes of a box grater or in a food processor fitted with a grating attachment. Combine with ½ teaspoon salt in a colander and let stand for 10 to 15 minutes. Gather it in your hands and squeeze out as much liquid as possible.

Place a medium skillet over medium heat. Add 1 tablespoon olive oil and, when hot, the shallot or onion. Cook until just softened, 2 to 3 minutes, then stir in the zucchini mixture. Cook until dried out slightly and beginning to caramelize, about 5 minutes more. Remove from the heat and stir in the nuts, zest, and several grinds black pepper. Season with salt.

Twist the mushroom stems to separate them from the caps and set the stems aside for another use—such as for vegetable stock or in the broth for the Miso Soba Bowl with Greens and Mushrooms (page 142). Use a teaspoon to fill the cavities with the filling, pressing it in, and arrange the stuffed mushrooms in a baking dish.

Combine the remaining 2 tablespoons panko and the cheese or nutritional yeast with a splash of olive oil in a small bowl. Sprinkle this mixture over the mushrooms. Drizzle the dish with a bit of olive oil, then bake for 15 to 20 minutes, until the mushrooms are tender and the topping is golden brown. Serve warm.

Certainly you can make soufflé just for one, but the theater of the thing is best suited for when you've got an audience. Invite your dinner guests into the kitchen when the dish comes out of the oven, or else they'll probably miss it in its fully risen glory. Summer squash seems destined for the soufflé treatment—its delicate flavor is a perfect match for the soufflé's delicate texture. As a light dinner, serve this with a simple green salad.

Summer Squash Soufflé

SERVES 4

2 tablespoons butter, plus more
    for greasing
½ cup finely grated Parmesan cheese,
    plus more for the pan
1 pound firm summer squash
    (about 3 small or 1 medium-large)
Salt

2 tablespoons all-purpose flour
½ cup milk
5 eggs, separated
Freshly ground black pepper
3 tablespoons minced parsley, chives,
    or dill, or a combination

Butter a 1½-quart soufflé dish (or another comparably sized dish—a shallow one works fine, but will cook faster and not yield as much rise) or 4 individual ramekins. Sprinkle the greased dish(es) with cheese, tapping and turning to ensure even coating.

Grate the squash using the fine holes of the box grater or similar insert in a food processor fitted with the grating attachment. Combine the grated squash with ½ teaspoon salt in a colander to drain for 10 to 15 minutes, then squeeze out as much excess moisture as possible.

Preheat the oven to 375°F.

In a small saucepan, melt the butter over medium heat. Sprinkle in the flour and stir with a whisk for a minute or two, until it smells nutty and has darkened a shade, then pour in the milk while whisking. Bring to a simmer and continue whisking until the sauce thickens to coat the back of the spoon. Cool for a few minutes. Stir in the egg yolks, cheese, drained zucchini, and a few grinds of black pepper.

Using a stand or hand mixer, beat the whites to stiff peaks, first ensuring that your bowl (preferably a metal one) is sparkling clean, with no trace of grease. Stir in a third of the whites, along with the fresh herbs, and then fold in the remaining whites in two batches. Transfer the mixture to the prepared dish(es). Bake until puffed and golden on top, about 30 minutes for a large soufflé, or 20 minutes for small ones. Don't open the oven to check on doneness until the last 5 to 10 minutes of cooking. The center(s) should be just barely jiggly, but definitely not liquid. Serve immediately.

If you've got a medley of summer squash to choose from—little baby zucchini and yellow squash, any of the round summer squash or pattypan varieties—this is a great way to use them up. Just cut everything into roughly the same thickness to allow it to cook evenly. This brightly flavored dish speaks of summer, but given our easy year-round access to summer squash, it's just as welcome a dish during cold months when you crave a flash of warm sunshine. It's a full meal served with some steamed rice or other grains on the side.

Summer Squash Green Curry with Tofu

SERVES 4

3 small or 2 medium zucchini or other
    summer squash (12 ounces total),
    sliced into ½-inch-thick pieces
1¼ teaspoons salt, divided
2 shallots, coarsely chopped
3 cloves garlic, coarsely chopped
1-inch piece ginger, peeled and coarsely
    chopped
1 or 2 serrano chiles, coarsely chopped
    (or ¼ teaspoon red pepper flakes)

¼ teaspoon sugar
1 tablespoon olive oil
Half of a 15-ounce block firm tofu,
    cubed
1 cup canned coconut milk
1 medium ripe tomato, chopped, or
    heaping ½ cup cherry tomatoes, halved
Zest and juice of ½ lime
½ cup coarsely chopped fresh herbs
    (basil, cilantro, chives)

Place the zucchini in a colander and toss it with ½ teaspoon salt. Let stand as you get started on the rest of the dish.

Combine the shallots, garlic, ginger, chile(s), sugar, and remaining ¾ teaspoon salt in a mini food processor and pulse until you have a paste, adding water by the teaspoon as necessary. Alternatively, combine in a mortar and pestle or pile on a cutting board and pound or chop to form a paste.

Warm the oil in a deep skillet or saucepan over medium-low heat. Add the paste and cook until very fragrant and darkened a shade from the caramelization, but not burnt, 12 to 15 minutes. Add more water by the tablespoon as it begins to stick to the pan.

Use a towel or paper towel to blot out as much liquid from the summer squash as possible. Add the zucchini to the skillet, followed by the tofu, coconut milk, and ½ cup water. Bring to a simmer and cook until the zucchini is tender, another 12 to 15 minutes (do a taste test). Stir in the tomatoes and cook for 2 minutes more.

Serve over cooked rice or grains, garnished with herbs and a wedge of lime per serving.

Every time I make this soup I'm surprised by how flavorful it is, given the notorious mildness of summer squash. Cashews and a bit of vinegar allow it to sing. It comes together easily, as a quick blender affair, and you can serve it warm, straight out of the blender, or chill it. If going the cold route, blitz in some additional water to thin it out before serving, as the soup will thicken as it sits.

Creamy Zucchini Soup, Hot or Cold

SERVES 4

¼ cup raw cashews
1½ pounds zucchini or other summer
    squash, cut into cubes
3 tablespoons olive oil, plus more
    for drizzling

1 tablespoon white wine vinegar
½ shallot, chopped
1 small or ½ large clove garlic
1 teaspoon salt, plus more as needed
Freshly ground black pepper

Place the cashews in a glass or bowl and cover with hot water. Let stand for about 20 minutes, until softened.

Pour about ½ inch water into a saucepan fitted with a steamer insert and bring to a simmer. Add the zucchini, cover the pan, and cook for about 4 minutes, until just tender. Transfer to a blender and add the remaining ingredients. Blend until smooth and, with the motor running, pour in water to thin the soup until your desired consistency is reached—anywhere from ½ to ¾ cup. Let blend for 30 or 45 seconds to achieve smoothest possible consistency. Season with salt and black pepper as needed.

For hot soup, serve immediately, as the just-steamed zucchini should have kept it hot (otherwise reheat it in a saucepan over low heat). For cold soup, cool to room temperature and then chill thoroughly in the refrigerator. If the cold soup is too thick, return it to the blender and thin with water. In both cases, garnish with a drizzle of olive oil and black pepper right before serving.

What if zucchini's tendency toward mushiness was an asset rather than a liability? That's where this dip comes in. After sautéing the vegetable and cooking out some of the water, you let it go beyond tender, to a consistency where it can be coarsely mashed with a spoon. Omitting the almonds, it can also be used as an omelet filling, or scooped over hot rice, or as part of an open-faced sandwich, draped with a nice melting cheese like fontina.

Mashed Zucchini Dip

MAKES ABOUT 2 CUPS

1½ pounds firm zucchini or yellow squash, cubed
½ teaspoon salt, plus more as needed
1 tablespoon olive oil

1 lemon
½ cup coarsely chopped basil
Freshly ground black pepper
¼ cup sliced, toasted almonds (optional)

Combine the zucchini and salt in a colander and let stand for about 15 minutes. Use a clean towel or a few paper towels to blot them dry.

Warm a wide skillet over medium heat and add 1 tablespoon olive oil. When hot, add the zucchini. Cook, turning it often, until it turns golden and the liquid that pools in the pan is mostly cooked off, 10 to 15 minutes. Deglaze with a long squeeze of lemon juice, scraping up the browned bits from the bottom of the pan, then remove from the heat. Use a potato masher or large fork to coarsely mash the squash, leaving a good amount of texture in there.

Transfer the zucchini to a medium bowl. Stir in the basil and a few grinds of black pepper. Add additional lemon juice and salt if needed. Serve warm or at room temperature, sprinkled with the almonds and drizzled with a bit more olive oil, with crackers and crudités alongside.

I hadn't yet acquired the palate for it, but as a kid I loved making beer bread with my mom because it was such an easy baking project—just a few ingredients, and soon enough it was perfuming the whole house with the comforting promise of fresh bread. Here's a variation on that classic, very simple recipe, in which summer squash marries with scallions and Parmesan to create something much more flavorful and a bit more decadent. You can leave out the cheese to make the bread vegan, or swap 3 tablespoons nutritional yeast if you'd like.

Savory Zucchini Beer Bread

MAKES ONE 8 ½ X 4 ½–INCH LOAF

2 medium zucchini or yellow squash
  (about 12 ounces total), coarsely grated
1 teaspoon salt, divided
¼ cup plus 1 tablespoon olive oil,
  plus more for greasing
3 cups all-purpose flour (substitute
  up to half whole-wheat flour)
1 tablespoon baking powder
1 tablespoon sugar

½ teaspoon freshly ground black pepper
2 scallions, green and white parts,
  thinly sliced
¼ cup coarsely shredded Parmesan
  cheese
2 tablespoons finely shredded Parmesan
  cheese
1¼ cups light and crisp beer, such as a
  lager, pilsner, or Kölsch

Toss the zucchini with ½ teaspoon of the salt in a colander and let stand for 15 minutes. Gather it up in your hands and squeeze out as much moisture as you can.

Preheat the oven 375°F. Generously grease an 8 x 4-inch loaf pan.

Whisk together the flour, baking powder, remaining ½ teaspoon salt, the sugar, and black pepper. Add the zucchini, scallions, coarsely shredded cheese , and ¼ cup of the olive oil, folding to combine, then pour in the beer. Let stand for a few minutes as the dry ingredients absorb the beer, then fold gently until everything is moistened. It'll be a dense and tacky batter. Scrape into the prepared pan.

Drizzle with the remaining 1 tablespoon olive oil and sprinkle with the finely shredded cheese. Transfer to the oven and bake until set in the center and a tester comes out clean, 75 to 80 minutes. Cool in the pan for 10 minutes, then unmold. This bread can be served warm (though it'll be a bit gooey inside) and should be eaten within a day or two, stored loosely covered at room temperature.

This dish is inspired by the Catalan tradition of drizzling honey over fried eggplant that my friend, the fantastic vegetarian cookbook author Hetty McKinnon, introduced to me. As an alternative to assembling and broiling the dish here, you can serve this as a solo course "modular" style: Arrange three or four zucchini halves on serving plates and spoon the marinara over, then drizzle with honey, dot with crumbles of goat cheese, and scatter with the basil to finish.

Honey-Baked Zucchini with Marinara and Goat Cheese

SERVES 4

8 tablespoons olive oil, divided
3 tablespoons honey, plus more
    for drizzling
Zest of 1 lemon
1½ teaspoons salt, divided
Freshly ground black pepper
8 small or 4 medium zucchini,
    halved lengthwise (about 2 pounds)

3 cloves garlic, smashed and minced
¼ teaspoon red pepper flakes
One 28-ounce can crushed tomatoes
½ cup crumbled goat cheese
    (4-ounce log)
Small handful basil leaves, thinly sliced,
    for garnish

Preheat the oven to 375°F. Line a baking sheet with aluminum foil.

Whisk together 6 tablespoons of the olive oil, the honey, lemon zest, 1 teaspoon of the salt, and plenty of black pepper in a large bowl. Add the zucchini halves and use your hands to evenly coat each piece, then arrange each piece facedown on the baking sheet. Transfer to the oven and bake for 12 minutes. Flip and bake for 5 to 7 minutes more, until tender and lightly golden. Switch the oven to broil on high.

Meanwhile, heat remaining 2 tablespoons olive oil in a medium skillet over medium heat. Add the garlic and red pepper flakes and stir for about 1 minute, until fragrant, then add the tomatoes and the remaining ½ teaspoon salt. Cook for about 15 minutes, until slightly reduced. Taste for seasoning.

Arrange the baked squash in a gratin dish, spoon the marinara sauce over, and top with the goat cheese and a light drizzle of honey. Broil for 3 to 5 minutes, until lightly browned and bubbling. Just before serving, scatter the basil on top. Alternatively, arrange the components on individual plates or a platter, without broiling, as directed in the headnote.

Here's a salad full of earthy flavors, with chickpeas and tahini framing the dish's profile. If you have access to a grill, use it to cook the zucchini spears—brushing them lightly with oil and cooking them over high, indirect heat—rather than broiling them. Some smoky char is a glorious flavor on summer squash. To serve as a solo salad course, leave the tahini out as you dress it, and instead pool about 2 teaspoons of the tahini over four plates and pile the dressed salad on top, as pictured. You can serve it warm, at room temperature, or cold.

Broiled Zucchini and Chickpea Salad

SERVES 4

1½ pounds zucchini or other
    summer squash (2 medium)
Olive oil
Salt
2 cups cooked chickpeas
    (one 14.5-ounce can, rinsed)
¼ red onion, sliced into strips

½ cup tender herb leaves, such as parsley,
    basil, cilantro, or dill
1 lemon
2 tablespoons olive oil
3 tablespoons well-stirred tahini
Freshly ground black pepper

Place an oven rack close to the heat source and preheat the broiler to high.

Quarter the zucchini lengthwise and arrange the spears on a baking sheet. Rub lightly with oil and sprinkle with salt. Place under the broiler and cook until blistered and tender, 5 to 7 minutes. When safe to handle, chop into chunks.

Combine with the chickpeas, onion, and herbs in a large bowl. Zest the lemon over the salad, then add the juice of about half of the lemon, the olive oil, tahini, ½ teaspoon salt, and several grinds of black pepper. Fold gently and add additional lemon juice or salt as necessary. Serve warm or at room temperature. Alternatively, plate the vegetables and chickpeas over a puddle of tahini, as directed in the headnote.

CHAPTER 15

Dessert Every Day

Home cooking deserves a bit of ceremony. This doesn't mean fine china, pressed linens, and coursed dishes (though I do believe that cloth napkins, in addition to minimizing the waste of disposable items, have a way of elevating a weeknight meal). Rather, I think that for a cook to enjoy cooking and, importantly, for it to be fully appreciated by those who are cooked for, there needs to be a sense of intention and an energy around the event that says: *Oh, here's what's happening—it's time to eat.* No one should take it for granted.

Try to sit down with the food and give it your attention. Resist the ideology that says eating is an activity built for multitasking. Submit yourself to an established pace, which will help to reinforce the ceremony. Perhaps the whole family sits down to eat, or you and your partner do, or as I did on and off for many years of happily living alone, you set a table for one. The food is dished, passed, acknowledged, enjoyed. Then the plates are cleared. I know this isn't always possible, not with young children and unrelenting jobs and any number of factors beyond one's control, but it's worth trying every now and then.

But even if dinner is a rushed and absentminded affair, what comes next has the promise of redemption: dessert. Bless! Dessert after dinner, something purely about pleasure, a literal sweet note to end the day on.

For me, a meal doesn't seem complete without dessert. My mouth waters for something sweet. Sure, this can sometimes be satisfied by a piece of fruit (especially when brightened up with one of the seasoned salts for seasonal fruits on page 234), but something homemade is usually the top choice. A scoop of ice cream with a warm topping spooned over, or a plate of cookies for the table to share, or even a few squares of chocolate and a handful of toasted nuts: All these things help usher the mind into understanding that the meal, and by extension, the day, is reaching its end. It eases the transition.

Some of these desserts can be thrown together in a few minutes and have been primed for weeknights—all of the ice cream toppings, for example. Others require a bit more planning, but still not much work. A few recipes—the biscotti and the galette—have been my go-tos for many years. Some, like the rosé-watermelon granita and the tea-spiced rice pudding, are new favorites. What they all have in common is that they add the final punctuation to a meal with a sweet note that lingers.

Toppings for Ice Cream

A dessert spoon and a tub of your favorite ice cream, whatever flavor or dairy-rich or dairy-free style it may be, is hardly lacking. It's a perfect dessert. But sometimes it's worth gussying it up with an easy and inventive topping, such as one of the ones that follow.

CANDIED GRANOLA CRUNCH

MAKES ABOUT 1½ CUPS

I've been making candied nuts to add to eighties-inspired spinach salads since I was a kid—where you melt the sugar in a skillet, and then, going as quickly as possible, stir in nuts before it hardens into a spun-sugar mass. Granola can be candied using the exact same method, and any flavor you like will work.

¼ cup sugar
1½ cups granola, your choice

Flaky salt

Place a skillet (preferably nonstick) over medium heat and add the sugar. Cook without stirring as the sugar begins to melt and turn amber—watch closely, as it'll turn quickly toward the end. Cook further, swirling once or twice, until it darkens a few shades to that of maple syrup and all the sugar has melted. Remove from the heat and immediately stir in the granola, using a rubber spatula and working quickly to coat it as evenly as possible. Spread it out on a plate to cool and sprinkle with a few pinches of flaky salt. After it's hardened, break into bite-size pieces before sprinkling over ice cream. Stored in an airtight container, it'll keep for a week.

CINNAMON-TOAST CRUMBLES

MAKES ABOUT 1 CUP

Here's what you'd get if you took cinnamon toast and ground it up like breadcrumbs. It needs to be made with coarsely ground, homemade breadcrumbs—the sandy, store-bought ones won't cut it. See page 182 for notes on breadcrumbs.

3 tablespoons butter or coconut oil
¼ cup coarsely chopped walnuts or pecans
1 tablespoon ground cinnamon

1½ cups plain, coarsely ground, dried breadcrumbs
¼ cup sugar
¼ teaspoon flaky salt

Melt the butter in a medium skillet over medium-low heat. Once the foaming subsides, add the nuts and cook, stirring frequently, until fragrant and the butter is beginning to brown, about 2 minutes. Add the cinnamon, then the breadcrumbs, and cook for 3 to 5 minutes more, until they've soaked up the butter and become crisp. Quickly stir in the sugar and salt, then remove from the heat. Cool for at least 10 minutes before serving. These will keep in an airtight container for a week.

MISO-BUTTERSCOTCH SAUCE,
PAGE 230

CINNAMON-TOAST
CRUMBLES,
PAGE 227

CANDIED GRANOLA CRUNCH,
PAGE 227

KOMBUCHA OR
SPARKLING WINE FLOATS,
PAGE 231

BLUEBERRY-LIME COMPOTE,
PAGE 230

BLUEBERRY-LIME COMPOTE

MAKES ABOUT 1 CUP

If you're in the habit of keeping frozen berries on hand, you're just a few minutes from an excellent ice cream topping. What sets this one apart from others is the step of fine-tuning the acid against the salt: taste carefully, adding spritzes of lime juice and small pinches of salt back and forth until suddenly the savory side of the blueberries zips into focus. A mix of berries, including raspberries, blackberries, and strawberries, works well here, too.

2 cups frozen blueberries

3 tablespoons sugar

Zest of 1 lime

1 tablespoon rum or brandy (optional)

Fresh lime juice

Salt

Combine the berries (no need to thaw them) and sugar in a small saucepan and place over medium heat. Cook until the mixture begins to simmer, the berries break down, and it thickens slightly, 5 to 8 minutes. Remove from heat and add the lime zest and rum or brandy, if using. Stir in a squeeze of lime juice and a pinch of salt. Taste, adjusting the salt and lime juice until the flavors come into bloom.

MISO-BUTTERSCOTCH SAUCE

MAKES ABOUT 1 CUP

The salty, umami character of miso adds something new and complementary to caramel and butterscotch, lending this dessert a bit of a savory underside. And the "scotch" in butterscotch of course refers to whiskey, but you can leave it out, especially since the miso is such an endearing wild card. This sauce is especially good over banana ice cream.

4 tablespoons butter

2 tablespoons smooth-textured white miso

½ cup brown sugar

¾ cup heavy cream

1 tablespoon whiskey (optional)

½ teaspoon flaky salt

Melt the butter in a small saucepan over medium heat. Add the miso and cook for 2 to 3 minutes, until fragrant and beginning to brown. Stir in the brown sugar and, once moistened, pour in the cream. Whisk to combine, bring to a simmer, then cook for about 8 minutes, whisking occasionally, until smooth and darkened a shade. Remove from the heat and transfer to a heat-safe jar or container. When cool, stir in the whiskey, if using, and salt.

KOMBUCHA OR SPARKLING WINE FLOATS

YIELD VARIES

This is a root beer float but for adults, and a recipe so simple a recipe is nearly redundant. But there's great opportunity in here to play around as you pair the flavor of ice cream with your beverage of choice. Gingery ice cream almost always pairs well with kombucha, and so do pear and other fruit sorbets. Vanilla and citrus-forward ice creams and sorbets go great with most sparkling wine.

Ice cream or sorbet (see headnote)

Kombucha or sparkling wine

For each serving, place a scoop of ice cream in a wine glass, tumbler, or sundae glass, then gently pour the kombucha or sparkling wine over the top. It'll foam up considerably. Serve immediately, with a spoon.

TAHINI MERINGUES

MAKES 15 SMALL MERINGUES

Even a crumbled store-bought meringue makes a delicious ice cream topping, adding some distinctive texture. But if you have a few egg whites left over, homemade ones are well worth the minor effort. These are inspired by the peanut butter pavlova in Alice Medrich's *Sinfully Easy Delicious Desserts*.

½ cup sugar

1 teaspoon cornstarch

2 egg whites

½ teaspoon lemon juice

Pinch of salt

2 tablespoons well-stirred tahini

¼ teaspoon vanilla

Preheat the oven to 280°F and line a baking sheet with parchment paper. Stir together the sugar and cornstarch in a small bowl.

In a very clean mixing bowl, or the one that fits into a stand mixer, combine the egg whites, lemon juice, and salt, and use the whisk attachment of the stand mixer or a hand mixer on medium-high speed to beat them to soft peaks. Working slowly while beating, add the sugar a spoonful at a time—after about 5 minutes, you should have a stiff, shiny, and thick meringue. Drizzle the tahini over the surface, then add the vanilla and fold a few times to combine, leaving some streaks intact.

Use a dessert spoon to make 15 golf ball–sized scoops of the meringue on the prepared baking sheet, spacing them apart by about 2 inches. Use a toothpick or paring knife to make decorative wisps and swirls if you like. Bake for about 40 minutes, until lightly golden and crisp to the touch. Cool completely. Crumble a cookie or two over ice cream to serve. In an airtight container, these will keep for about a week.

I learned this biscotti method working as a prep cook during college. It seemed crazy to me: An industrial-size mixer bowl filled with a mixture that looked like very dry sand that we'd add eggs to one by one until it very, very slowly coalesced into a cookie dough. (Every cookie I'd ever made was done in the reverse—dry ingredients added to wet.) But they were hands-down the best biscotti I've ever had, full of toasty, caramelized flavor, and with *snap*— such a perfect accompaniment to a cup of coffee. It took me years to scale down and figure out how to make them at home, and I'm pleased to share it here. Filling options are endless: add dried fruit, like cherries and mandarins, or chopped chocolate, or different types of toasted nuts. Add a bit of instant espresso powder, or ground cinnamon, or fennel seeds, or even the spice blend garam masala.

Polenta and Pine-Nut Biscotti

MAKES ABOUT 45 COOKIES

1 cup sugar
3 tablespoons butter, softened
½ teaspoon vanilla extract
2 cups all-purpose flour
⅓ cup polenta, preferably stone-ground

1 teaspoon baking powder
½ teaspoon baking soda
½ teaspoon salt
2 eggs
⅔ cup pine nuts

Preheat the oven to 350°F. Line a baking sheet with parchment paper.

In the bowl of a stand mixer fitted with the paddle attachment, beat together the sugar and butter on medium speed until the mixture is light and soft and the butter is fully incorporated, 1 to 2 minutes. Beat in the vanilla. Add the flour, polenta, baking powder, baking soda, and salt and continue mixing on medium-low speed until well combined—it'll be a very dry mixture. With the mixer running, add one of the eggs and mix well, then add the other. It'll seem like the dough won't ever come together, but after 60 seconds or so, the dry mixture will moisten and cohere. (If after a few minutes you've lost hope, add a teaspoon of water or egg white to assist.) With the mixer on low speed, stir in the pine nuts.

Divide the dough into two pieces. On a clean work surface, roll each piece into a log about 12 inches long. Transfer to the prepared baking sheet, then flatten it down slightly so that it's a rectangle about 2 inches wide. Repeat with remaining portion of dough, placing it on the baking sheet with at least 4 inches between the two pieces, as they'll spread as they bake. Transfer to the oven and bake for 30 to 40 minutes, until lightly browned and set in the center, turning the pan once halfway through. Cool completely.

Reduce the oven temperature to 250°F. Line a second baking sheet with parchment paper.

Place the biscotti logs on a work surface and use a serrated knife to slice them diagonally into pieces about 1 centimeter thick. Divide the cookies between the prepared baking sheets, standing them upright on their bases (this allows both sides to toast so that you don't have to flip them halfway through). Transfer to the oven and bake for about 50 minutes, rotating the pan halfway through, until crisp. Cooled completely, the biscotti will keep, stored in an airtight container, for at least a week.

Seasonal fruit—citrus, melon, stone fruit . . . the stuff that's sweet and juicy and ripe—can function as a beautiful dessert when arranged simply on a plate with a few little piles of seasoned salts to pair each bite with. This is admittedly a light dessert, one to be enjoyed on hot nights and/or to follow rich meals.

Seasoned Salts for Seasonal Fruit

MAKES ABOUT 2 TABLESPOONS OF EACH SALT

Seasonal fruit

Ancho Chile–Lime Salt
4 teaspoons flaky salt
1¼ teaspoons ancho chile powder
Zest of 1 lime

Serve with: Mango, pineapple, papaya, peaches, apricots

Fennel Salt
4 teaspoons flaky salt
1 teaspoon fennel seeds, crushed
Zest of 1 lemon

Serve with: Peaches, apricots, watermelon, cantaloupe, citrus rounds or supremes

Sumac Salt
1 tablespoon ground sumac
1 teaspoon flaky salt

Serve with: Watermelon, cantaloupe, honeydew, mango, pineapple, citrus rounds or supremes

TO MAKE THE ANCHO–CHILI LIME SALT: Preheat the oven or toaster oven to 225°F.

Mix all the ingredients together in a small bowl and use your fingers to thoroughly incorporate the zest into the salt. Spread out on a small piece of parchment, place on a baking sheet, transfer to the oven, and bake until the citrus is dry, 15 to 20 minutes. Cool, then store in an airtight container. The flavors are best if used within 2 weeks.

TO MAKE FENNEL-PEPPER SALT: Preheat the oven or toaster oven to 225°F.

Mix all the ingredients together in a small bowl and use your fingers to thoroughly incorporate the zest into the salt. Spread out on a small piece of parchment, place on a baking sheet, transfer to the oven, and bake until the citrus is dry, 15 to 20 minutes. Cool, then store in an airtight container. The flavors are best if used within 2 weeks.

TO MAKE SUMAC SALT: Stir together both ingredients in a small bowl. Store in an airtight container. This blend will keep for months.

Cut the fruit into small, easy-to-handle wedges or spears. Scatter the salt(s) on a small plate or saucer. To eat, gingerly sprinkle the salt onto pieces of the fruit, bite by bite.

This is a light, tender cake—with a thin pool of pudding on the bottom! I wasn't familiar with this category of dessert until I encountered a chocolate pudding cake in Jeanne Lemlin's book *Simply Satisfying.* It comes together very quickly, is best served right out of the oven, and really needs to be topped with ice cream. The fresh ginger adds a good jolt of heat; if that isn't appealing, feel free to omit it.

Gingery Maple Pudding Cake

SERVES 6 TO 8

1 cup all-purpose flour
2 teaspoons baking powder
1 teaspoon ground ginger
½ teaspoon ground cinnamon
½ teaspoon salt
6 tablespoons butter, melted
¼ cup maple syrup

1 egg
1 teaspoon vanilla extract
1 tablespoon grated fresh ginger (optional)
⅓ cup brown sugar
½ cup boiling water
Flaky salt
Vanilla ice cream, for serving

Preheat the oven to 325°F.

Whisk together the flour, baking powder, ground ginger, cinnamon, and salt in a large bowl. In a tall measuring glass, whisk together the butter, maple syrup, egg, vanilla, and fresh ginger, if using. Add the wet ingredients to the dry ingredients, whisking until just combined. Spread the batter into an 8 x 8-inch baking pan (no need to grease it) and sprinkle evenly with the brown sugar. Pour the boiling water over the top—don't stir! Transfer to the oven and bake for 18 to 25 minutes, until puffed and set in the center. Sprinkle with a few pinches of flaky salt, let cool for about 10 minutes, then serve with ice cream.

Once you get used to making the crust, a galette really does come together quite quickly: mix together the dough, chill it in the fridge while you toss together the fruit in that same bowl, then roll out the crust and assemble; it can sit in the fridge for a few hours before baking. All kinds of seasonal fruit are great in galettes: apples, pears, plums, all manner of berries, peaches, nectarines, figs, quince. If it's a fruit that tastes good cooked, it will taste good in a galette. Serve warm (with ice cream or whipped cream) or at room temperature.

Fruit Galette

SERVES 6

Crust

1 cup all-purpose flour
1 tablespoon sugar
½ teaspoon salt

6 tablespoons cold butter, cut into cubes
3 to 5 tablespoons ice water

Filling and assembly

3 cups sliced fruit (plums, peaches, apples)
    and/or fresh or frozen berries
4 tablespoons sugar, plus more for dusting

Pinch salt
1 tablespoon all-purpose flour

Prepare the crust: Stir together the flour, sugar, and salt, then add the cold butter and toss to combine. Use your fingers to rub the butter into the flour, pinching it between your thumbs and fingers until you've got a ragged mixture with irregular pieces of butter still intact, the largest about the size of an almond. Sprinkle 3 tablespoons of the ice water over the mixture and use a fork to quickly incorporate. Keep adding water by the ½ tablespoon until it appears just moistened—a dough that's too wet will lead to a tough crust, so err on the side of it seeming a little dry. Dump the mixture onto a piece of plastic wrap. Working from the outside of the plastic, shape it into a flat disc. Wrap, then refrigerate for at least 30 minutes and up to overnight.

Preheat the oven to 375°F.

Prepare the filling (use the same bowl as for the crust): Combine the fruit, 3 tablespoons of the sugar, and the salt in a large bowl. In a small bowl, stir together the flour and remaining 1 tablespoon sugar.

Place the chilled dough on a lightly floured work surface and roll into a circle about 13 inches in diameter. Roll from the center, rotating 90 degrees after each roll, and adding a bit more flour as needed if the dough sticks. Drape the rolled dough over a rolling pin and transfer to a parchment-lined baking sheet. Spread the flour-sugar mixture evenly over the dough, leaving a clean rim of about an inch, and pile the fruit on top. Fold the crust around over the fruit, pleating rustically as you go. Brush the exposed pastry with water, then sprinkle generously—over the crust and the fruit, too—with sugar. Transfer to the oven and bake until the fruit juices are bubbling in the center and the crust is golden, 50 to 60 minutes, or more depending on the fruit.

Serve warm, with fresh whipped cream or ice cream, or cold, perhaps for breakfast, with yogurt.

Here's a sweet, comforting cup of tea but in rice pudding form. There are so many ways to make rice pudding—and it's fascinating that so many cultures have their own spin on the dish—but this treatment has a looser consistency and less dairy than many recipes, which allows the flavor of the rice and the spices in the tea to shine. Experiment with the tea: green tea and chamomile both make wonderful substitutes.

Tea-Spiced Rice Pudding

SERVES 4

⅓ cup short- or medium-grain white rice
⅔ cup water
2 spiced black tea bags, such as chai
1½ cups milk
¼ cup sugar
Pinch salt
½ teaspoon vanilla extract

¼ cup heavy cream (optional)
Optional garnishes: pinches of cinnamon or gratings of nutmeg, shavings of dark or unsweetened chocolate, tart fruit like berries or pomegranate seeds, citrus supremes, crumbled biscotti (page 232) or other crisp cookies

Combine the rice and water in a medium saucepan and swish around to ensure that no grains adhere to the pan. Discard the paper tags from the tea bags and add them to the pan. Place over medium heat and bring to a simmer. Cook until the water level dips just below the rice, 3 to 5 minutes. Carefully pick out the tea bags, pressing them against the side of the pan with a spatula to extract all the liquid from them, then add the milk, sugar, and salt to the pan. Bring to a gentle simmer and cook until thick and creamy and the rice is very tender, 20 to 25 minutes. Stir often to prevent scorching and to ensure that the milk doesn't bubble over, especially toward the end. Remove from the heat and stir in the vanilla.

The pudding can be served warm, as is. Or to serve cold, chill for at least 4 hours. Just before serving, whip the cream, if using, until soft peaks form, then fold it into the pudding. In either case, serve unadorned or with garnishes of choice.

My friend Blake Bachmann is an incredibly inventive cook and also a rosé fanatic—he and his sister Laura make rosé under the label Rose & Thistle in Napa, California, and it's one of my most favorite wines to drink. He devised a genius method for making frosé (a frozen-rosé concoction) made primarily from frozen cubes of watermelon, which gives the drink delicious texture and is so quenching that some of my friends and I think it has a sobering effect. That frosé led to this idea for granita, a dead-of-summer dessert that can be enriched with dollops of yogurt or whipped cream, if you like, or is perfect served plain. If you've ever made granita before, you know that one traditional step is to "rake" the mixture with a fork every hour or so as it's freezing, to help the mixture to freeze evenly and give it a light texture. Here, by using alcohol (wine and a small amount of gin), the mixture never freezes solid—so you only have to scrape it once, just before you serve it.

Melon and Rosé Granita

SERVES 6 TO 8

¼ cup sugar
6 cups cubed seedless watermelon,
    cantaloupe, or honeydew
1 cup rosé

2 tablespoon gin
Juice of 1 lime
Plain yogurt, coconut yogurt, or softly
    whipped cream, for serving (optional)

Stir together the sugar and ¼ cup hot water in a small bowl until the sugar dissolves. Add the syrup and the remaining ingredients to a blender or food processor (in batches, if necessary) and blend until smooth.

Place a 9 x 13-inch baking pan into the freezer, and then pour the mixture into it (this spares you the perilous step of traversing your kitchen while carrying a wide, sloshing dish full of liquid). Leave it there for at least 8 hours, until fully frozen. Just before serving, scrape the mixture all over with a fork to create a light texture of icy shards. You can return the "raked" mixture to the freezer for another hour or so if you aren't ready to serve, but any longer than that and you'll need to rake it once more. Serve immediately out of the freezer, before it melts, with a dollop of yogurt or whipped cream, if desired.

Acknowledgments

Start Simple is in large part motivated by the great pleasure I take in sharing meals and cooking with my brother and his family—Max, Casady, Zoe, and Ali. It is dedicated to you all. Since I first started conceiving the book, the goal was to create healthy, delicious, and doable recipes that just might fit into your very busy and never-boring lives. I hope that I succeeded!

Thank you to my agent, Alison Fargis at Stonesong Literary, for being an invaluable champion of me and my work for several years now—I honestly don't think I'd have been able to sustain this career were it not for you. And thank you to my editor, Julie Will at Harper Wave, for believing in *Start Simple* and investing in it with your ideas, resources, and collaborative spirit. Thanks also to designers Milan Bozic, for the vibrant and pitch-perfect cover, and Leah Carlson-Stanisic, for an interior design that elegantly and seamlessly brings to life some fussy concepts that I grappled with in Word doc format. Thank you as well to assistant editor Haley Swanson and publicist Yelena Nesbit—what incredible luck to work with such an accomplished and capable team.

I got to collaborate with such an amazing group of visual thinkers on the photos for this book. Thank you, Cara Howe—I love working with you, and after so many years of being on jobs together here and there, *Start Simple* feels like a crowning achievement (so far!). Prop stylist Paige Hicks is a household name in the food photography world and for good reason—thank you for all your beautiful work here. Thanks as well to Christine Bronico, for bringing so much skill and infectious good energy, and David Wilson, for your help in the kitchen. Thanks to Hetty McKinnon and Jodi Moreno, proprietors of Neighborhood Studio in Brooklyn, for creating such a gorgeous gorgeous kitchen set and workspace. Thank you to Le Cruset and Misen, for generously providing some of your beautiful products for us to incorporate into the photos.

Thank you, Allira Tee, for your absolutely perfect illustrations—they established the visual tone for this book in such a big way!

Thank you to my friends and colleagues, who do such astonishingly good and important work, and have been so supportive of mine, that it sometimes keeps me awake at night: Chitra Agrawal, Liz Alpern, Blake Bachmann, Cathy Erway, Gabriella Gershenson, Anna Hezel, Alicia Kennedy, Caroline Lange, Ben Mims, Wendy Rex Meilke, Matt Robard, Mayukh Sen, Nik Sharma, David Tamarkin, Michael Harlan Turkell, and Ora Wise. Thank you to Steve Viksjo, my partner at *Jarry*, for your friendship and collaboration on one of the most rewarding projects of my life. And thanks to my writing group, for always being encouraging and having incisive feedback: Emily Gould, Bennett Madison, Laura Waterman, and Anya Yurchyshyn.

Thank you to Kate Chiasson and all the fabulously talented cooks at Stonewall Kitchen Cooking School, for inviting me to teach cooking classes—where I workshopped many of the recipes that appear here.

Thank you as always to my "coven" of close friends, whom I couldn't live without: Meghan Best, Lesley Enston, Izzy Forman, Crista Freeman, and Kat Hunt.

Thank you to my stepmom, Pam, and my stepsiblings, Anna, James, Mary Kathryn, Nick, and Luke, not least of all for getting me through the first stage of the Broken Ankle Incident of Thanksgiving 2018, but also for making family gatherings full of life and fun.

Thank you to my dad. Repairing and recovering from my broken ankle forced me to take a break (get it?) from my life for a few months in the winter of 2018–19, when I was supposed to be finishing this book but couldn't do much beyond lay in bed in a druggy haze with my foot propped up on a pile of pillows. Unprompted, Dad came from North Carolina to New York to sleep on an air mattress in my living room, to schlep groceries on the subway like a New Yorker, and to help take care of me for a period of several weeks when I had absolutely no idea how badly I needed it. It's had a profound impact on me, the full-scale gesture of it. Thank you, Dad, for that and for your continued support of everything I do. I love you.

And Vincent, whatever twist of fate it was that made our lives collide has made my life immeasurably better. I love knowing you, love living with you, and love sharing adventures with you. Thank you for always enjoying whatever I cook, even on the (very rare) occasions when I'm not on my A-game.

Index

Index

Index

Index

Index

About the Author

LUKAS VOLGER is the author of three previous cookbooks, including *Bowl* and *Veggie Burgers Every Which Way*. He cofounded and serves as the editorial director of the award-winning queer food journal *Jarry*, and previously founded the small-batch, premium veggie burger line Made by Lukas. His accessible, whole foods–based approach to vegetarian cooking has been featured in the *New York Times*, *Time*, and *The Splendid Table*, among other print, radio, television, and online publications, and his writing occasionally appears on Taste and Epicurious. He lives in Brooklyn, New York. For more information, follow @lukasvolger on Instagram or visit LukasVolger.com.

Lukas Volger is the author of *Bowl* and *Veggie Burgers Every Which Way*. He is also the cofounder and editorial director of *Jarry*, an award-winning independent magazine that explores where food and queer culture intersect, and previously founded Made by Lukas, a Brooklyn-based line of premium veggie burgers. His work and writing have been featured in the *New York Times*, *Vogue*, the *Washington Post*, the *Boston Globe*, and other publications, and on *The Splendid Table*, Epicurious, and Food52.